This notebook belongs to:

....

Robert M. West

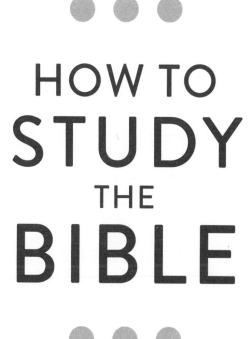

HOW TO STUDY THE BIBLE

Notebook & Organizer

BARBOUR BOOKS

An Imprint of Barbour Publishing, Inc.

Published by Barbour Books, an imprint of Barbour Publishing, Inc., P.O. Box 719, Uhrichsville, Ohio 44683, www.barbourbooks.com.

Our mission is to publish and distribute inspirational products offering exceptional value and biblical encouragement to the masses.

Member of the
Evangelical Christian
Publishers Association

Printed in China.

DEDICATION

• • •

To the men of God I've known
throughout my life who have
taught me how to study the Bible

CONTENTS

• • •

INTRODUCTION

• • •

When you study the Bible, you'll discover what millions of people have found throughout the centuries: you're reading the Word of the living God. In times past, He spoke to His special servants audibly, in visions, in dreams; now His main method of revelation to all humanity is His written Word.

Over a period of fifteen hundred years, the Holy Spirit directed forty holy men of God, living on three continents, to write His words into sixty-six books using three different languages. These writings were preserved and collected into the single volume we know as the Bible.

Though people wrote it, the Bible itself says God was its ultimate source. In 2 Timothy 3:16 (KJV), we read, "All scripture is given by inspiration of God," which literally means it was breathed out by God.

The New Testament gives several descriptive titles to the Bible: the Word of God, the oracles of God, the Word of Christ, the holy scriptures, the word of truth, and the word of life. In studying the Bible, we're learning God's Word, holy and true, which contains the knowledge of eternal life.

The people of Thessalonica (who received two letters from the apostle Paul, which became part of the Bible) recognized that the apostle was giving them the Word of God in his preaching and from his pen. First Thessalonians 2:13 (NASB) tells us, "For this reason we also constantly thank God that when you received the word of God which you heard from us, you accepted it not as the word of men, but for what it really is, the word of God."

Years ago, when I was a high school student, my reading skills were poor. I had difficulty understanding and retaining what I read. Later, when I realized that God communicates to us through His written Word, I concluded that if I wanted to know Him and His truth, I must give myself to studying His Word. I've studied the Bible for many years now, encouraged along the way by devoted Christians who love the Bible.

Many Christians have made this same decision, and virtually all will testify to the great spiritual blessings that come from studying God's Word. Having studied and taught the Bible now for more than thirty years, I'll share things I've learned through my own experience as well as what others have taught me.

My hope and prayer is that through reading this book, you'll be encouraged to become one of those believers who is taught by God, learning His Word and receiving the special blessings He has reserved for you.

If you're new to the Christian faith, you'll find helpful recommendations in this book. If you've been a Christian for a while but have struggled in your personal Bible study, you'll be encouraged and challenged to have victory in this area of your life. If you're reading this book as a mature believer established in Bible study, my intention is to stir you up—to remember those things you have already learned and to help others learn how to study God's truth. People in your life need to learn what God has taught you, and you can become an answer to their prayers for a person to help them.

Some may rationalize their lack of Bible study by saying that life is too busy or studying the Bible is too hard. Others, who struggle with sin, as I did early in my Christian life, may honestly admit that it's just too convicting to read. Please don't let excuses stop you from studying God's Word.

Jesus made it clear that learning and living the Bible is God's will for our lives. He said, "Man shall not live by bread alone, but by every word that proceeds from the mouth of God" (Matthew 4:4). Bible study isn't just a nice thing to do—it's essential to our lives!

PREPARATION

● ● ●

READYING OUR HEARTS FOR BIBLE STUDY

*For the word of God is living and active and sharper than
any two-edged sword, and piercing as far as the division
of soul and spirit, of both joints and marrow, and able
to judge the thoughts and intentions of the heart.*

Hebrews 4:12 NASB

People who want to learn how to study the Bible often ask, "Where do I begin?"

It's a good question, but the answer might be surprising. We actually begin with ourselves. We prepare our hearts to study the Bible.

Many activities in life require preparation. If we're going to exercise, we first stretch our muscles to avoid injuries. If we're going to do a job around the house, we first gather the tools and materials the job requires. If we're going on a trip, we first make sure our car is properly maintained, that we've packed everything we need, and that we have a good map.

We might be tempted to think we can just jump in without any kind of preparation, but we've all experienced what happens when we fail to prepare: problems and disappointments.

Studying the Bible also requires some preparation so that we can have a profitable time studying and avoid problems that might discourage us, leading us to give up. I'm talking about personal preparation that focuses on our hearts. This is something we can easily overlook, and not addressing it contributes to the breakdown of daily Bible study.

Frequently the Bible uses the word *heart* in a figurative sense, referring to the innermost portions of our being—our thoughts, emotions, and will—rather than the physical heart. It's our hearts that interest the Lord. When the prophet Samuel was preparing to anoint the future king of Israel, the Lord told him, "Man looks at the outward appearance, but the LORD looks at the heart" (1 Samuel 16:7).

As we think about personal Bible study, we shouldn't view it as another intellectual exercise like the study of math, science, history, or anything else that interests us. When studying these disciplines, the mind is engaged, but not the heart. God wants us to increase our knowledge of His Word with our minds, but He also intends for the power of His Word to affect our hearts and that our lives will be changed to become more like Christ's.

Concern for a change of life was expressed by the Lord Jesus for His disciples when He prayed, "Sanctify them by Your truth. Your word is truth" (John 17:17).

Two disciples, who didn't recognize the resurrected Lord Jesus as He walked with them on the Emmaus Road, illustrate the experience of having the heart involved in learning God's Word. As they walked with Jesus, He began to teach them things about Himself from all of the Old Testament scriptures. Later that evening, as they recalled their experience, they said to each other, "Did not our heart burn within us while He talked with us on the road, and while He opened the Scriptures to us?" (Luke 24:32).

The hearts of these two disciples had previously been confused and discouraged as they thought the crucifixion of Jesus meant His defeat and end. When they finally recognized Him and He vanished from their presence, they considered how their hearts were warmed with spiritual revival and excitement. The spiritual heartburn they experienced was a good thing!

When our minds and our hearts are prepared and involved in Bible study, our time spent in God's Word is enjoyable and exciting.

People can have a good study Bible, have a few helpful study books, follow numerous recommended procedures, and have a quiet place to concentrate, and still not benefit spiritually from the time spent in the Bible because their hearts aren't prepared to be involved in the process. Their focus may be on only intellectual growth, not spiritual growth.

The religious leaders in Jesus' day, the scribes and Pharisees, made this error. They had a serious heart condition known as hypocrisy. Jesus described them this way: "These people draw near to Me with their mouth, and honor Me with their lips, but their heart is far from Me" (Matthew 15:8).

They were the kind of people who go through the motions of religious activity, more concerned about their artificial, external religious rules than about having their hearts right before God through faith and obedience to His Word. The human heart, described as "deceitful above all things, and desperately wicked" in Jeremiah 17:9, is of major concern to God.

This chapter opened with the words of Hebrews 4:12. The context of this verse reveals that God knows everything about every one of us. As we read His Word, it functions as an X-ray machine or heart monitor, revealing to us what He sees in our hearts. Let's see ourselves as God sees us. His Word exposes our hearts so we can take corrective action (Hebrews 4:13).

Addressing issues of the heart was something that most of the scribes and Pharisees neglected to do, but Ezra, an Old Testament priest, "prepared his heart to seek the Law of the LORD" (Ezra 7:10). That's what we need to do as we begin Bible study.

I suggest that preparing our hearts means three things. First, we need to approach God's Word with reliance. Second, we need to approach God's Word with resolve. And third, with repentance.

RELIANCE

● ● ●

RELY ON THE HOLY SPIRIT

Many people who begin to study the Bible will soon be saying, "I need help!" That's a good conclusion to come to. We all need help, and the person to help us is God. He gave us His Word and also assists us in understanding it. The technical term for this help is *illumination*. Let's look at a few New Testament verses describing God's work illuminating people's hearts.

On one occasion Jesus was teaching people about His Father's work in the lives of those who would be saved. He quoted the Old Testament when He said, "It is written in the prophets, 'And they shall all be taught by God' " (John 6:45). People who have come to know the Lord have experienced the illuminating work of God in their minds and hearts to understand their own lost, sinful condition and to see that Christ is the solution to their problem.

Paul spoke about illumination when he said, "But the natural man does not receive the things of the Spirit of God, for they are foolishness to him; nor can he know them, because they are spiritually discerned" (1 Corinthians 2:14).

The *natural man* refers to someone who hasn't been saved and therefore doesn't have the indwelling Holy Spirit. People in this condition reject the Gospel message and view it as foolishness. Subjects such as sin, guilt, forgiveness, grace, and salvation don't make sense to them and don't have personal value. They don't have interest, understanding, trust, or appreciation for Christ and His Word because they haven't had the work of God's Spirit in their hearts. Christ's Word must be understood on a spiritual level, not just an intellectual level.

Even the apostles needed divine help for understanding. Before the risen Lord Jesus returned to heaven, He assisted them in understanding the Old Testament. "And He opened their understanding, that they might comprehend the Scriptures" (Luke 24:45). Even though these men learned the scriptures throughout their lives, they failed to understand all that the Word of God predicted about Jesus. They needed His help to finally see.

John Newton, the author of the beloved hymn "Amazing Grace," wrote in the lyrics of that song, "I once was lost but now am found, was blind but now I see." He was referring to his own experience of not grasping biblical truth as a person who was spiritually lost. When he was saved by God's grace, his spiritual blindness was healed so he could say, "Now I see."

The only person who can make the blind see is God, so He's the One we depend on to give us understanding of His Word. The first thing a person needs, simply put, is to be saved, to be totally dependent on God for all his or her spiritual needs. (See Acts 16:30-31.)

Once we have recognized our need for help from God to understand His Word, we should regularly pray for His assistance. The psalmist realized this and expressed his dependence on God: "Open my eyes, that I may see wondrous things from Your law" (Psalm 119:18). This is a great prayer for us as well when we prepare our hearts to study His Word.

We should give great concern to our dependence on the Holy Spirit. Not only does He seek to enlighten us, but He also reveals that the enemy of our souls is trying to influence our study of God's Word and lead us astray: "In latter times some will depart from the faith, giving heed to deceiving spirits and doctrines of demons" (1 Timothy 4:1).

RELY ON MATURE BELIEVERS

Not only should we rely on the teaching ministry of the Holy Spirit, but we should also rely on mature believers who have a strong knowledge of God's Word.

According to the apostle Paul, God gives certain people a supernatural ability to teach the Word: "Having then gifts differing according to the grace that is given to us, let us use them. . .he who teaches, in teaching" (Romans 12:6-7). But teaching occurs in many settings, as Moses told the ancient Israelites: "These words, which I am commanding you today, shall be on your heart. You shall teach them diligently to your sons and shall talk of them when you sit in your house and when you walk by the way and when you lie down and when you rise up" (Deuteronomy 6:6-7 NASB). The design of God is that mature Christians teach His Word to others.

Just before He ascended into heaven, Jesus gave His apostles their final instructions, telling them, "Go therefore and make disciples of all the nations, baptizing them in the name of the Father and the Son and the Holy Spirit, *teaching them to observe all that I commanded you*" (Matthew 28:19-20 NASB, emphasis added). What Jesus commanded is recorded for us in the Bible—and the Holy Spirit and gifted teachers help us to understand and apply those commands to our own lives.

RESOLVE

• • •

By saying we must study the Bible with resolve, I mean we should be determined to do this and have clear in our minds why we are spending part of our day studying. This is another part of personal preparation. We'd know why we were studying if we were to give a devotional message or share our thoughts about a biblical topic with a group. We'd be motivated by the specific task before us.

But what we're considering at this point are the reasons we're to be consistent in our everyday study habits. What is it that motivates us to be determined to study like the Berean Christians in Acts 17:11, who "searched the Scriptures daily"?

The best answers come straight from the Bible. The following sections describe what God would have us keep in mind so we'll be motivated to be faithful in our study. Call these the Top Ten Reasons for Personal Bible Study.

1. To settle the issue of our own salvation

Paul reminded Timothy about Timothy's own experience: "From childhood you have known the Holy Scriptures, which are able to make you wise for salvation through faith which is in Christ Jesus" (2 Timothy 3:15). This is the primary issue that needs to be settled in everyone's life.

God uses His Word as a means to save sinners. As we think about our conversion, we may be able to identify Bible verses that God used in our lives to save us—or at least a believer's life-giving words that were based on scripture. God also wants us to have what the hymn writer Fanny Crosby called "blessed assurance." Many Christians experience doubts about their own conversion, and through learning those portions of scripture that address this subject, we can have a deepening confidence about our own salvation.

When people want to start reading the Bible, a good place to begin is the Gospel of John in the New Testament, because this book was specifically written so people might read about Christ, believe in Him, and receive the gift of eternal life from Him. (See John 20:30-31.) This book of the Bible was written with the purpose of helping those who read it find salvation in Christ.

2. To grow spiritually

New Christians are sometimes described as babes in Christ, and of course, all babies need to grow. Peter gave this instruction to Christians in the early church: "But grow in the grace and knowledge of our Lord and Savior Jesus Christ" (2 Peter 3:18).

He also gave a direct exhortation that they should have the same kind of desire for the basic truths of God's Word that a newborn baby has for milk. "As newborn babes, desire the pure milk of the word, that you may grow thereby" (1 Peter 2:2). This is a picture representing intense hunger for God's Word so that we can grow in our understanding and spiritual strength. The Bible repeatedly refers to itself as food for the soul. Just as our bodies need food to survive, our souls need the spiritual food of the Bible.

In Ephesians 4, Paul expressed the same concern as Peter for the growth of believers. He didn't want them to be tossed about and carried away with every wind of doctrine; he wanted them to be steady and strong. When we neglect to develop our understanding of truth, we can be more easily influenced by the error of false teachers. Spiritual growth through studying the Bible protects us from bad spiritual influence.

3. To receive personal blessing and encouragement

Paul wrote, "For whatever things were written before were written for our learning, that we through the patience and comfort of the Scriptures might have hope" (Romans 15:4). As believers, we often experience discouragement in our Christian walk. A common cause of this discouragement is conflict between believers, which Paul addresses in Romans 15. Difficulties between Christians, which create a lack of unity, can be discouraging. As we all eventually learn, there's no lack of tension and trouble in local churches. But as we study the Bible, we see Christ's example. How He interacted with people is the pattern we're to follow for living and for treating others.

When we study the Bible, we'll also read numerous promises God made to give believers hope, and stories about how God providentially worked in the lives of people. Meditating on all these passages of scripture encourages us to persevere in our own Christian life with comfort and hope. "Great are the works of the LORD; they are studied by all who delight in them" (Psalm 111:2 NASB).

Discouragement can also come from conviction about our sins as we're brought face-to-face with God's holy standards in the Bible. When we're honest about our lives, we have to admit we fall short of His glory. It's frustrating to struggle with the same sins over and over, not being able to break bad habits in our lives. But as we continue to read God's Word, we'll also discover the comfort and hope available to us through God's mercy, grace, and forgiveness in Christ.

We can learn about His power to transform our lives and conquer our sinful habits by the power of His Word. Reading about how He pardoned and delivered others—and then us—gives us hope. The God of patience and comfort wants us to be encouraged. Since the Bible was written for our education, the more we learn, the more we can be encouraged.

4. To receive personal guidance

When faced with many of life's decisions, we often wonder, *What should I do now?* Learning the Bible can be helpful in answering this question. "Your word is a lamp to my feet and a light to my path" (Psalm 119:105). The psalmist pictured the effect of learning God's Word as having a lamp for life that lights the way before us so we can see where we're going.

As the nation of Israel journeyed in the wilderness after their exodus from Egypt, they were led by a pillar of fire at night and a pillar of cloud by day. That was how God worked for that group of people at that time. What God has provided for us in our journey is His written Word, which gives us the light of knowledge and wisdom to follow.

Many times the Bible addresses our specific situation, but when it doesn't, there are principles we can apply to our lives so we have confidence that we're being led by God's Word.

In Psalm 119, the psalmist refers to his daily experience of living in a world filled with spiritual and moral darkness, a world that calls good evil and evil good. As believers concerned with pleasing God and wanting to do His will, we try to make decisions that honor Him, but the influence of a dark world often makes this difficult. Through studying the Bible we learn what the will of God is and experience His direction.

As we seek God's guidance, He'll lead us by His Spirit (Romans 8:14), which always agrees with what God has revealed to us in His Word. His Spirit's leading never contradicts what He has written. If our personal decisions contradict what has been written in the Bible, then we can be sure we aren't being led by God.

5. To defend ourselves against the devil

Soon after we become Christians, we find out that the Christian life involves spiritual warfare. In Ephesians 6, Paul instructs believers with these words: "Put on the whole armor of God, that you may be able to stand against the wiles of the devil" (verse 11). The wiles of the devil are the methods he uses against people, trying to keep them from doing the will of God.

The Christian's defense against this assault is putting on the spiritual armor of God: Christian character and lifestyle empowered by God's Spirit. A vital part of this armor is "the sword of the Spirit, which is the word of God" (verse 17).

When the devil confronted Jesus in Matthew 4:1-10, tempting Him to act independently of God's will and questioning God's provision, protection, and plan, Jesus used God's Word to defend Himself. Three times in this story when the devil tempted Him, Jesus responded, "It is written," and then quoted specific verses from Deuteronomy to rebuff the temptations. Jesus was able to draw from His knowledge of the Old Testament to overcome temptation by His knowledge of, trust in, and obedience to the Word. So if you're going to say to the tempter, "Get behind me, Satan!," remember to finish your sentence like Jesus did—with an appropriate text of scripture that counters his temptation.

In the apostle John's first letter, he refers to a group of young men, saying, "You are strong, and the word of God abides in you, and you have overcome the wicked one" (1 John 2:14). These believers withstood the devil's assault through their knowledge and application of scripture.

Through Bible study, we'll also be able to remember specific Bible verses, and by applying them, we'll be able to overcome the devil's temptations.

6. To effectively teach God's truth to the next generation

Deuteronomy 6:4-9 is known to Jews as the *Shema* (Hebrew for *hear*, the first word of the passage), and devout Jews recite it twice daily. It gives instruction about loving God, loving His Word, and loving our children by teaching them God's Word. "And these words which I command you today shall be in your heart. You shall teach them diligently to your children, and shall talk of them when you sit in your house, when you walk by the way, when you lie down, and when you rise up" (Deuteronomy 6:6-7). Parents teaching their children is God's pattern for the Christian home.

Parents aren't simply to teach their children, but to teach them diligently. The text also reveals that the teaching is informal, given throughout the day, inside and outside the home. Parents are the primary teachers of their children, and they can only do this effectively if they first learn God's Word themselves.

Parents are to have answers for their children when questioned about God's Word. Moses confirmed this when he wrote, "When your son asks you in time to come, saying, 'What is the meaning of the testimonies, the statutes, and the judgments which the LORD our God has commanded you?' then you shall say to your son. . ." (Deuteronomy 6:20-21). Parents have only a limited amount of time to teach their children before the children are grown and begin their own lives. I can testify that the time, although it's years long, goes by quickly. So studying the Bible ourselves helps us in this important task.

7. To be able to counsel others

God wants to use us to provide knowledge about what He has said in His Word to others. "Let the word of Christ dwell in you richly in all wisdom, teaching and admonishing one another" (Colossians 3:16). In time, God wants to use you to help others who may be newer to the faith. We might be able to remember with gratitude and fondness older Christians who helped us when we wondered what the Bible said about a particular subject.

We should notice what Colossians 3:16 says about learning the Bible: The Word of Christ is to "dwell in you." This literally means to be at home in you. The Word of Christ is to take up residence in us, influencing every part of our lives. The text goes on to say that the Word should "dwell in you richly in all wisdom," indicating that we're to have a full understanding of the Bible. Then we can be a good friend providing wise counsel.

8. To be ready to speak with unbelievers about Christ

"But sanctify the Lord God in your hearts: and be ready always to give an answer to every man that asketh you a reason of the hope that is in you" (1 Peter 3:15 KJV). The concern of Christians shouldn't be winning arguments but winning people. We should be able to answer questions when we're asked and to give an explanation about our faith. Some people who won't listen to a sermon may want to find out about Christ in a private conversation, and we're told to be ready. The more we learn through studying, the more effective we'll become in sharing God's truth with others.

9. To verify that the teaching of others is the truth of God

One group of early Christians, the Bereans, stood out from the rest. "They received the word with all readiness, and searched the Scriptures daily to find out whether these things were so" (Acts 17:11). They checked in scripture to confirm that what Paul taught them was true. They were so committed to this that they did it daily. It's a mistake for us to accept the message of Christian teachers just because they're humorous, dynamic, on television or radio, or have written books. The content of their message must be true, and it's good for us to validate it from our own study. Bible teachers should never be offended that people do this; they should encourage it.

10. To present ourselves approved to God

"Be diligent to present yourself approved to God as a workman who does not need to be ashamed, accurately handling the word of truth" (2 Timothy 2:15 NASB). Learning God's truth involves the work of studying.

Like divers who work to locate pearls in the ocean or miners who labor to find gold in the earth, Christians are workers who study the Bible to discover God's truth. We live our lives before God, and as servants we're to regularly present our lives to Him to be examined. We hope to have a sense of His approval and eventually hear from Him, "Well done, good and faithful servant." Divine approval comes from diligently studying God's Word so we can accurately apply it to our own life and share it with others.

Having examined these ten reasons for studying the Bible, we now need to ask ourselves, *How many of these reasons are a thoughtful part of my life and motivate me in the study of God's Word?* All ten reasons are very important in the Christian life: Many relate to our personal spiritual growth and whether we experience abundant life. The others relate to how we bless other people.

If you need to improve in this area of "studying the Bible with resolve and purpose," pray and ask God to continue the good work He has begun in your heart of teaching you His truth.

REPENTANCE

● ● ●

Since the beginning of time, sin has brought horrible effects into people's lives. Some of these effects have found their way into our time of studying God's Word.

Two scripture texts specifically describe the necessity of removing our personal sin so that it doesn't hinder our growth in our Bible study time. Repentance is changing our mind about our sin, which should lead us to take action against it. Sad to say, there is no shortage of sin in our lives—so we dare not ignore this aspect of preparing ourselves for Bible study. The comprehensive instruction found in Proverbs 28:13 surely applies here: "He who covers his sins will not prosper, but whoever confesses and forsakes them will have mercy."

The first text specifically related to Bible study speaks about our *desires*. First Peter 2:2 states that we should, "as newborn babes, desire the pure milk of the word, that [we] may grow thereby." Please notice that *before* we can desire the Word in such a way that we can grow spiritually, 1 Peter 2:1 states that we must deal with sin in our lives. We're instructed to "lay aside" or rid ourselves of specific sins such as malice, deceit, hypocrisy, envy, and evil speaking. We can imagine this "laying aside" as the taking off of dirty clothes to be replaced by clean ones.

The point of 1 Peter 2:1-2 is clear: sin will cloud our understanding and erode our desire for the Word. When people are sick, their appetite is often affected— they don't feel like eating. The same thing happens in our Bible study: we just won't feel like spending time in God's Word when our sin has not been dealt with.

The second Bible text speaks of personally *receiving and applying* what we study. James 1:21 encourages us to "receive with meekness the implanted word." Once again, notice that the beginning of this verse emphasizes the importance of first dealing with our sin. We're to "lay aside all filthiness and overflow of wickedness." Before there can be a *receiving*, there must be a *removing*.

Some scholars have noted that the word "filthiness" in verse 21 in the original Greek text, when used in a medical context, has a connection to *earwax*. When wax builds up in the ears, it hinders hearing and must be removed. That meaning illustrates how removing sin can improve our "hearing" of God's Word.

James's letter is addressed to believers called "beloved brethren" who have already had the Word "implanted" in their hearts (verses 18-19), and they must learn this truth about removing sin if they are to become "doers of the word" (verse 22). That's exactly where Bible study should lead us.

When we approach God's Word in reliance on Him and more mature believers, we're progressing toward successful Bible study. When we approach His Word with the resolve of knowing God and His ways better, we're also making strides toward successful study. When we draw near to His Word with repentance, we're removing obstacles that hinder successful Bible study. God's Word is truly "living and active," ready to change us from the inside out.

INTERPRETATION

● ● ●

DISCOVERING WHAT THE BIBLE MEANS

---

*Be diligent to present yourself approved to God as
a workman who does not need to be ashamed,
accurately handling the word of truth.*

2 TIMOTHY 2:15 NASB

I vividly remember my high school history teacher responding to a student who had just misquoted the Bible in an attempt to prove a point in a classroom discussion. The teacher said, "You can make the Bible mean anything you want it to mean." Even at that young age, I was left with the impression that the Bible should be understood carefully, not carelessly.

Frequently people discussing the meaning of the Bible say, "Oh, that's just your interpretation." Is there a way to figure out what it means? The answer is a resounding yes! In this chapter, I'll share a number of guidelines to help you interpret the Bible properly.

Whether we realize it or not, we all interpret the Bible whenever we try to understand its meaning and make applications to our lives. The fact that we're already doing this shows how important it is that we learn to interpret correctly.

ONE INTERPRETATION, MANY APPLICATIONS

● ● ●

A good thought to begin with is this: each verse of scripture has only one intended meaning even though there may be many applications. The Bible isn't written to mean different things to different people. Some fast food restaurants tell their customers, "You can have it your way!" That might be true when buying burgers, but it's not true when trying to understand the Bible. The issue in every verse is always what *God* means by it, not what it means to me.

When interpreting a biblical text, there are a number of things to consider. Some texts clearly apply to everyone everywhere, while other texts apply only to people in the Bible who lived in a former time. Some things are to be understood literally, and others figuratively.

Some people bring their personal circumstances to texts of scripture and may wrongly think that God is speaking directly to them in some mysterious and secret way from a particular text.

You may have heard the anecdote about the man who opened his Bible and pointed to a verse, hoping God would give him a personal message where his finger landed. He happened to place his finger on Matthew 27:5 and read, "He. . .departed, and went and hanged himself."

Perplexed about what this meant for him, he tried again, turning to another section, and his finger landed on Luke 10:37: "Then Jesus said to him, 'Go and do likewise.' "

Starting to get nervous, he tried again. Turning to John 13, he placed his finger on verse 27: "Then Jesus said to him, 'What you do, do quickly.' "

This funny story illustrates some people's casual and mystical approach to understanding the Bible.

In a personal experience, one day I had a doctor's appointment to get test results on what had the potential to be a serious ailment. That morning, I spent time in prayer and Bible study, and I happened to be reading Jeremiah 46. When I came to verse 11, I read these words: "In vain you will use many medicines; you shall not be cured."

Now if I hadn't learned how to interpret the Bible, this would have been a troubling verse. But it wasn't a direct, mystical message from God to me. It was actually addressed to the "daughter of Egypt," and I was glad! Later that day I received good news from the doctor, which confirmed to me that properly interpreting the Bible can save us from unnecessary anxiety.

Poor interpretation comes from preconceived ideas, bad theology, hastiness in reaching conclusions, and ignorance of principles of interpretation. This is why it's so important to learn basic guidelines that help us learn what God means by what He said.

WORTH THE INVESTMENT

● ● ●

You may think you're getting into more work than you want to do, but I encourage you to overcome the temptation to think that it won't be worth it. Some of the best time we spend in our lives will be spent studying the Bible. This isn't just tedious academics, but the examination of a love letter, the message of a God who loves us. Realizing this makes the time we spend studying enjoyable.

The time and work you invest will be rewarded by great discoveries of precious truth. Miners who search for gold or other precious metals keep their minds fixed on the value of the discovery they hope to make. They know they must devote time to their task.

If you hear about a microwave Bible study plan—that is, a plan that lets you get it done quickly—my advice is to ignore it, because it won't be that beneficial. The slow cooker study plan is much better: the one that goes slowly, requiring a greater time commitment, but resulting in greater discoveries.

It's been said that the Bible wasn't written for scholars, but for sinners. It's a book for all of us. Many parts are more difficult than others, but this shouldn't discourage us. Even Peter said that some of the things written by his beloved brother Paul were hard to understand (2 Peter 3:15-16).

A wise pastor once told me as I was beginning to learn God's Word that Bible study is like lifting weights. We start out lifting light weights and eventually work our way up to heavy weights. As we read and study the Bible, we don't have to be overly concerned by those things we don't understand. To switch the metaphor, all we need to do is grab the cookies from the shelf we can reach. As we read God's Word daily, we will grow in understanding and be able to deal with more difficult doctrines later.

WATCH OUT FOR FALSE TEACHERS

● ● ●

As a warning to those who want to understand God's Word, the Bible speaks of false teachers who manipulate what the Bible says and who can be a bad influence if we don't guard ourselves against them. Jesus criticized the Sadducees of His day, who denied physical resurrection. "You are mistaken, not knowing the Scriptures" (Matthew 22:29). These men explained away certain Old Testament texts and spiritualized others, resulting in serious error. Jesus also confronted the scribes, also known as lawyers, who were viewed as experts in the Mosaic law—yet they failed to understand the scriptures correctly themselves and were guilty of hindering others who were trying to learn God's truth (see Luke 11:52).

Paul spoke of some religious and educated people living in the last days when he said that they are "always learning and never able to come to the knowledge of the truth. . .these also resist the truth" (2 Timothy 3:7-8).

False teachers often redefine biblical words, so we must check to make sure we understand how they are using them or God's intended meaning of verses becomes lost.

Peter described how some people misuse God's Word with horrifying results. He said, "Untaught and unstable people twist [Paul's words] to their own destruction, as they do also the rest of the Scriptures" (2 Peter 3:16). These people play fast and loose with the scriptures, ignoring proper principles of interpretation.

Since we live in the day where there's a battle for the truth, it's important for Christians to be discerning about books, programs, and teachers. I'm glad for all Bible-believing Christians who've had great influence on the world through the media, but we should always be cautious, because it's difficult at times to tell who are wolves in sheep's clothing (Matthew 7:15).

Though there is agreement on the fundamentals of the faith by true believers, there are also in-house debates. Unfortunately, Christians who know the Lord and handle the Bible accurately still have disagreements about what certain passages of the Bible mean. This has resulted in division among Christian individuals and Christian denominations. Differences exist over the nature of the Bible, the age of the earth, divine election, eternal security, gifts of the Spirit, the ritual of baptism, and the timing of the rapture, just to name a few.

Differences between believers will exist until the Lord returns. At that time, He will answer all questions and unify all believers. Until that day comes, we must do our best to love the brethren we disagree with and learn how to interpret the Bible as well as we can. An ancient saying has its place here: "In essentials, unity; in nonessentials, liberty; in all things, charity."

INDUCTIVE BIBLE STUDY

● ● ●

In learning to interpret scripture, we must discuss inductive Bible study, which seeks to discover the facts and details in a text and to draw conclusions about the meaning of a text from those observations. Inductive study has a sequence of three components: observation, interpretation, and application.

- Observation answers the question, What does it say? What is the actual content in the text?

- Interpretation answers the question, What does it mean? Our task is to discover the original intent and meaning of the author.

- Application answers the questions, What does it mean to me? and How does it apply to my life?

When we use this sequence, we'll find information and ideas that might have been overlooked otherwise. When this type of study isn't practiced, the door to interpretive abuses opens.

OBSERVATION

Observation always comes first. Before we consider what a text means, we must ask what it says. This means reading and rereading a text until we become acquainted with it. Occasionally, after I've taught about some part of the Bible, people have asked me with surprise, "How do you get all of that out of one verse?" Part of the answer is learning to be observant.

Most of us have watched television shows where a crime scene is being investigated. The area is taped off, and the authorities begin looking for clues. As clues are found—a footprint or a piece of clothing, perhaps—the detective places a bright marker at the location. A trained eye takes in many clues. Pictures are taken of the scene to be studied later. Evidence is taken to the lab, where even more information is revealed. Many people are involved in a slow process to discover the truth about what happened. This is observation, discovering all that can be found.

As a kid, I grew up watching *Dragnet*, a police show. One of the main characters was Detective Joe Friday. One of his trademark statements was "Just the facts, ma'am." He wasn't interested in opinions or feelings. All he wanted was factual evidence. During the observation stage, we're also looking for the facts.

In developing our observation skills, we'll find it helpful to ask a series of questions. We can use them for any text. Put your text under a light and interrogate it! We just want the facts. Texts will have answers for most of the following questions.

- Who? Who was writing? To whom was the message originally written? Who are the people involved in the scenario?

- What? What's happening? What's said? Is it a command, an exhortation, a rebuke, a question, an answer, a prayer, a quotation of other scripture, something else? What's the main point? What key words or phrases are used? What's the context? What literary style is being used? Is it narrative, conversation, parable, prophecy, poetry, a letter, or a sermon?

- When? Are there time references? Are there words related to the past, present, or future? Look for words like *after*, *until*, *then*.

- Where? Are any locations mentioned—towns, roads, rivers, mountains, regions, or other landmarks?

- Why? Are there any clues about why things are being said or done?

- How? Is there an explanation about how things are done?

These six questions help us gain information to see what a text actually says.

INTERPRETATION

The ultimate interpretation question is, What did God mean by what He said? Interpretation is determining the meaning of a text once all of the facts are in. Compiling evidence from our observation takes some time, and we must guard against jumping to premature conclusions. New evidence can influence our conclusions, so we shouldn't be too hasty in moving to this part of the inductive process. We can see a clear example of this in the judicial system where some verdicts have been overturned when advances in DNA testing provided new evidence.

Some of us have been in Bible study classes where the facilitator asked, "What does this passage mean to you?" before the group observed the facts and determined what the author intended. This is a good question when asked at the right time because it forces people to think about the Bible, but it's not a good question to ask first because people speak offhandedly before they give thought to the text. In this situation, interpreting the Bible becomes totally subjective, meaning different things to different people.

But every verse in the Bible, generally speaking, means only one thing—what the original author intended—and that's what we're trying to discover. Interpretation of the Bible isn't a matter of personal opinion, feelings, or democratic agreement; it's a matter of gathering evidence from the text and following established principles of interpretation. Some people innocently make the error of reading a text, skipping interpretation altogether, and jumping to application.

John MacArthur tells the story of one of his assistant pastors, who counseled a couple who married as a result of a sermon preached on the destruction of Jericho. The pastor at a previous church had taught that God's people claimed the city, marched around it seven times, and the walls fell down. Then he explained to the young men that if a man believed God had given him a particular single young woman, he could claim her, walk around her seven times, and the walls of her heart would fall down! Of all the lessons to be learned about the fall of Jericho, lessons about marriage aren't among them.

Second Timothy 2:15 (NASB) speaks of "accurately handling the word of truth." In Greek, accurately handling literally means "cutting a straight line." When Paul, a tent maker, wrote to Timothy, he may have had in mind cutting material in a straight line to sew pieces of a tent together. Paul and Timothy needed to be precise and accurate in interpreting and teaching the Bible so it would all fit together without contradiction. They were to cut straight or handle straight the word of truth. Shame waits for those workers who mishandle the word of truth.

When we're trying to discover the meaning of the text, many times it's plain; it's on the surface of what we read. Alistair Begg, of the radio program *Truth for Life*, speaks repeatedly about "the main things and the plain things" when studying the Bible. Focus first on what is clear and obvious.

David Cooper, founder of the Biblical Research Society, established the golden rule of interpretation. The short version is, "If the plain sense makes good sense, seek no other sense or it will result in nonsense." Apply his rule first and work from there. Don't sacrifice plain meaning for unique, mystical, or obscure ideas.

Once we have asked the six observation questions of the text, we then apply six principles of interpretation.

1. The literal principle

The literal principle means interpreting the Bible with the normal meaning of words while recognizing figures of speech like symbolism, allegory, and metaphor. God has communicated with us through written language, so we should understand the words of scripture the way we use them in everyday life. Let a text speak for itself. When Jesus was born, it was a literal virgin birth. The miracles He performed were real. His death and resurrection were actual historical events.

We recognize that many portions of scripture, especially poetry and prophecy, are filled with figurative language. Psalm 91:4 is an example of figurative language in Hebrew poetry: "He shall cover you with His feathers, and under His wings you shall take refuge." This doesn't mean that God has feathers and wings; rather it provides an image of God as our protector the same way a bird protects its young by covering them with its wings.

A prophetic example comes from Revelation 1:16: "He had in His right hand seven stars, out of His mouth went a sharp two-edged sword." Literal interpretation doesn't suggest seven actual stars or a real sword. The symbolic meaning of the stars is explained in Revelation 1:20, while the meaning of the sword is found in Revelation 2:16 and 19:15.

Also in prophetic scripture, the "law of double reference" needs recognition. Bible scholar J. Dwight Pentecost explains the term: "Two events, widely separated as to the time of their fulfillment, may be brought together into the scope of one prophecy. This was done because the prophet had a message for his own day as well as for a future time." An example is Hosea 11:1, which refers to Israel's actual exodus from Egypt—though this same reference is quoted in the New Testament, seven centuries later, to refer to Mary, Joseph, and the baby Jesus fleeing to Egypt to escape the wrath of King Herod (Matthew 2:14-15). In this text is seen both historical and literal meanings along with the prophetic.

The literal principle—which certainly allows for poetic and prophetic under-standings—makes the Bible much easier to understand. There's no need to un-cover hidden meanings. Read and study the Bible like you would a letter from a friend—since that's what God has provided for us. Enjoy His Word in its most normal meaning.

2. The historical principle

The Bible must be understood in its historical setting before it can be fully under-stood in our contemporary setting. Bible students now become historians. We want to discover the original intent of the author by asking, *What did he mean by what he wrote?* Would our interpretation make sense to the first recipients? Before we ask what a text means to us, we first must ask what it meant to the original audience.

It's helpful to investigate the lifestyle and customs of that day, such as foot washing (1 Timothy 5:9-10), praying on a housetop (Acts 10:9), and girding the loins (1 Peter 1:13). Learning about the political and social backgrounds sheds light on certain texts. The Bible study tools mentioned in chapter 4 will prove helpful when studying historical background.

3. The contextual principle

The contextual principle means we should interpret a verse by the verses that sur-round it. You may have noticed that some verses begin in the middle of a sentence, so it's best to at least go back to the beginning of the sentence to get the flow of the author's thought. Some Bible teachers have said that context is so important that a verse of scripture should never be read by itself; it should always be read in its context to get the author's intended meaning.

The reason for this stance is summarized in this adage: A text out of context becomes a pretext for a proof text! In simpler words, this means a Bible verse standing alone can be misunderstood or misused to prove an error.

When Satan tempted Jesus and suggested that He should throw Himself down from the top of the temple, the devil quoted Bible verses out of context, giv-ing them a wrong meaning. A psalm about trusting God was twisted into meaning that it's all right to test God (Matthew 4:5-6 and Psalm 91:11-12). Jesus corrected the devil's error by quoting another text that rectified the wrong idea (Matthew 4:7 and Deuteronomy 6:16).

The following scriptures provide other examples of verses taken out of context—and therefore misunderstood:

- Matthew 7:1 (NASB) is a commonly quoted passage that says, "'Do not judge so that you will not be judged.'" This is often used to overlook or defend sinful behavior as some say that the Bible teaches we are not allowed to judge other people. Yet later in the passage, a lot of judging must be done in order to obey what Jesus says in verses 3-6! Matthew 7:1 actually prohibits a sinful judging—questioning thoughts or motives and judging prematurely, harshly, or unfairly—rather than true discernment, which Jesus encouraged in John 7:24. In the latter passage, Jesus actually told people to judge—but righteously.

- In an attempt at humor, 1 Corinthians 15:51 has been placed on some church nursery schedules to refer to babies. In part, it reads, "We will not all sleep, but we will all be changed" (NASB)!

- Some have used Jeremiah 10:3-4 to argue against the modern holiday custom of decorating Christmas trees. But the context clearly indicates the prophet was condemning *idolatry* (see verses 8 and 11, and a majority of the book of Jeremiah).

It's best to get the big picture of a text, then zoom in on the context, and finally the details. This is starting with the bird's-eye view and going down to the worm's-eye view.

- Find out the general theme of the book.

- Determine the emphasis of each chapter and how it relates to the book theme.

- Find the paragraph divisions and how they relate to the thrust of each chapter.

- Dig into the verses to get each one's main idea and how they relate to each other.

- Go deeper into verses by doing word studies.

This digging makes our conclusions much more accurate.

4. *The compatibility principle*

The basic premise of the compatibility principle is to compare verses or passages of scripture with other scripture to see how they fit together. The best commentary on the Bible is the Bible, so we let it interpret itself. Properly understood, the Bible doesn't contradict itself; it complements itself with an amazing harmony. If our interpretations contradict what the Bible says elsewhere, we need to change our conclusions. As we study a text or subject, other portions of scripture shed light on it for fuller understanding. For example, doctrinal truth is spread throughout the Bible.

I remember the first time I seriously read the Gospels, the first four books of the New Testament. I read Matthew, then Mark. By the time I had completed Luke, I knew I had read its stories before—and I had, in Matthew and Mark. I eventually learned that these books all present the life of the Lord Jesus, giving different details to provide a complete picture of His life. The four authors were like a quartet harmonizing. They were singing the same song but hitting different notes. Comparing scripture with scripture is a safeguard against error and contradiction.

5. *The grammatical principle*

It shouldn't surprise us to learn the grammatical principle has to do with grammar and sentence structure. Recognizing parts of speech and the way they relate to each other can reveal a lot about a biblical text. This is called *syntax*. It's been said that grammar and syntax are a lot like broccoli—you know it's good for you, but you'd rather not eat it. *Every* student of scripture must learn to use the grammatical principle. You'll learn to love it!

Seven easily overlooked but important key words that reveal clues to accurate meaning are *therefore, and, but, that, for, because,* and *if*. Examples of these are found in Romans 11-12.

In Romans 12:1, Paul writes, "I beseech you *therefore*, brethren, by the mercies of God, that you present your bodies a living sacrifice" (emphasis added). When we see the word *therefore*, we need to find out what it's there for. Find out what thoughts have gone before. In the first eleven chapters of Romans, Paul has laid the great foundation of the mercies of God by describing in detail God's plan of salvation. Paul then draws his thoughts to a practical conclusion in 12:1 and begs the Romans to present themselves to God as dedicated servants. He connects his practical appeal to his lengthy description of God's plan by the word *therefore*.

Verse 2 continues: "*And* do not be conformed to this world, *but* be transformed by the renewing of your mind, *that* you may prove what is that good and acceptable and perfect will of God." *And* introduces an addition, *but* points to a contrast, and *that* is used to begin a conclusion. Paul adds another appeal after his first one in verse 1 by using the word *and* at the beginning of verse 2. Then he presents a contrast with the word *but*. Paul exhorts believers not to succumb to external pressure to live and think like the unbelieving world, *but* to be internally transformed by renewing their thought life. (By the way, the source for renewed thinking is the Bible. See Psalm 1:1-2.)

That (along with *for* and *because*) is used to introduce a purpose or reason at the end of verse 2. The reason for having our thinking renewed and our life transformed is so we can have confidence that we know and are doing the will of God.

In verse 19, the word *for* is also used to introduce a reason: Paul has written that Christians shouldn't be vengeful *for* the scriptures say we shouldn't.

An example of the use of *because*, also used to introduce a purpose or reason, is found in Romans 11:20: "*Because* of unbelief they were broken off."

If is used in Romans 12:18: "*If* it is possible, as much as depends on you, live peaceably with all men." This word is used when a condition is present. Paul's point here is that Christians are always to be peacemakers, and if there is a lack of peace between a Christian and another person, it should never be the Christian's fault.

Considering these seven key words helps us better understand the structure and meaning of a text.

6. The Christological principle

Jesus Christ is the main theme of the entire Bible, so keeping an eye out for references to Him as we study is important. The ministry of the Holy Spirit is to point us to Christ. "But when the Helper comes. . .the Spirit of truth. . .He will testify of Me" (John 15:26).

Jesus said to unbelieving Jews of His day, "You search the Scriptures, for in them you think you have eternal life; and these are they which testify of Me. . . . For if you believed Moses, you would believe Me; for he wrote about Me" (John 5:39, 46). Moses wrote the first five books of the Old Testament, so we look for Christ there.

At the end of His earthly ministry, Jesus told His apostles, "All things must be fulfilled which were written in the Law of Moses and the Prophets and the Psalms concerning Me" (Luke 24:44). Therefore, we also look for Jesus in the prophetic books and the psalms.

One day, an Ethiopian eunuch was reading the Old Testament text of Isaiah, which contains a prophecy about the Lord Jesus. A believer, Philip, helped him understand what he was reading. "Then Philip opened his mouth, and beginning at this Scripture [Isaiah 53:7-8], preached Jesus to him" (Acts 8:35). We should always be looking for Christ.

APPLICATION

Now we come to application, the third component of inductive Bible study. This answers the question, How does this passage apply to me? Bible study doesn't end with interpretation; it continues to the question, So what? The goal of Bible study isn't only gaining information but also experiencing transformation. We're not just trying to get through the Bible; we're letting the Bible get through us. If there's a good example, follow it. If there's a warning, heed it. If there's a command, obey it.

If there's a promise, believe it.

Jesus prayed for all believers just before He died: "Sanctify them by Your truth. Your word is truth" (John 17:17). This is Jesus' request to God the Father that He use His Word to influence believers to live lives set apart for His purposes. Our lifestyle is to be affected by the Bible as well as our beliefs, and this requires a humble response of doing the will of God.

James said that what should characterize believers is being "doers of the word, and not hearers only" (James 1:22). Self-deception is talking ourselves out of obeying the Bible and therefore cheating ourselves out of the blessings of God that accompany obedience. Some people mark their Bibles, but their Bible seldom marks them.

Jesus spoke of the blessing of obedience and the foolishness of self-deception when He ended the Sermon on the Mount. He described two types of people, the obedient and disobedient, as builders. The obedient are like the man who built his house on a rock, which was able to stand when the storm came. The disobedient are like the man who built on a foundation of sand and experienced the destruction of his house when the storm came (Matthew 7:24-27). These two people both heard the truth but responded differently. One only learned it, while the other truly lived it.

Paul states in 2 Timothy 3:16 that scripture is inspired by God and is beneficial for four things, three having a practical emphasis: "All Scripture is given by inspiration of God, and is profitable for doctrine, for reproof, for correction, for instruction in righteousness." Paul is saying scripture is valuable for learning information to believe, for using as the perfect standard of right and wrong, for being restored after we've sinned, and for remaining restored. These four benefits are to make believers complete so that they can do whatever God has called them to do (verse 17).

Interpreting the Bible, then, includes the six observation questions, the six interpretation principles, and the necessary application to our lives.

CLASSIFICATION

● ● ●

EXAMINING BIBLE STUDY METHODS

*Now [the Bereans] were more noble-minded than those in
Thessalonica, for they received the word with great eagerness,
examining the Scriptures daily to see whether these things were so.*

ACTS 17:11 NASB

As the Berean believers studied the scriptures in an attempt to verify the truthfulness of Paul's preaching, they were thorough in their approach to God's Word and more than likely using some of the study methods that I'll suggest in this chapter. All methods of Bible study have value in learning God's Word, but whatever method we use, the point to remember is that studying the Bible is what's important. It's to our benefit to pursue the habit of daily reading and studying God's Word.

The usefulness of knowing a variety of Bible study methods is that it helps us be flexible in our approach to scripture as we concentrate on a particular text, subject, or even a word. It also contributes to balancing our learning.

BALANCE

● ● ●

Before we look at different methods of Bible study, some thoughts about being balanced in our study are appropriate.

OLD TESTAMENT/NEW TESTAMENT

I highly recommend balance in Bible study by using a variety of methods. For example, time spent studying the New Testament should be balanced by study of the Old Testament. It's not surprising that believers living under the new covenant want to spend their time in the New Testament learning about Jesus Christ and His Gospel, but the Old Testament is quoted in the New Testament about 250 times. It's been said, "The new is in the old contained, and the old is in the new explained."

When the Bereans were searching the scriptures, they were studying the Old Testament. The New Testament was in the process of being written at that time. Early Christians had a solid foundation of Old Testament truth, and New Testament truth was added as it gradually became available. This is what's meant by the idea that God's revelation has been progressive.

The amazing preacher Apollos is an example of a person receiving progressive revelation. His preaching from the Old Testament was powerful and accurate as far as it went, but his knowledge was limited. Aquila and Priscilla, believers who heard him teach, shared more of God's revelation with him, and Apollos grew to become more effective in serving Christ (Acts 18:24-28).

DOCTRINE/CHRISTIAN LIVING

Another area is balancing the study of Bible doctrine with the study of practical Christian living and how to apply doctrinal truth to everyday life.

Paul's preaching did this. He said to the Ephesian elders, "I have not shunned to declare to you the whole counsel of God" (Acts 20:27). The "whole counsel of God" is an all-inclusive term related to God's revelation covering both doctrine and duty in the Christian life. There was no subject that he intentionally omitted from his teaching. His preaching was well rounded because, in part, he wanted his hearers to be the same.

This is how our study should be so we gain a wider spectrum of truth and a good foundation of understanding we can build on.

Some Christians seem content to only occasionally study those things that spark their interest, while others have a diet of the latest Christian books that hit the bestseller list. My intention isn't to be critical of popular Christian books, for all pursuit of truth is helpful, but I'm concerned about poor study habits that sometimes neglect using the Bible altogether.

The point needs to be made that we should be involved in a balanced Bible study plan that uses a variety of techniques. In physical health, eating only those foods that we might enjoy—like snacks and sweets—won't contribute to good health. A balanced diet is required. This is equally true when we study the Bible.

SIX IMPORTANT BIBLE STUDY METHODS

● ● ●

1. The Expositional Method

Expositional Bible study means studying the Bible verse by verse and using the observation, interpretation, and application guidelines from chapter 2. The benefit of this method is that it reveals the flow of the author's thoughts throughout any text of scripture, which contributes to a more accurate understanding of individual verses.

No verse is to be left out as insignificant. Every verse contributes something to the overall idea in every section of scripture—that's why God put it there. It's our mission to discover the meaning.

For example, the verses before and after John 3:16 are not as well-known but are just as important. The expositional method does require more thinking about how verses relate to each other but also leads to greater understanding in the long run.

In Deuteronomy 12:32, God gave us an important lesson: "Whatever I command you, be careful to observe it; you shall not add to it nor take away from it."

In a way, the expositional method of study is like assembling a puzzle—every verse is like a piece of the total picture. If one piece is left out, the picture is incomplete. But when every verse is understood in its proper place, God's marvelous picture can be fully enjoyed.

Bible commentaries are helpful in pursuing the expositional method of Bible study.

2. The Survey Method

The importance of this study method has been well stated by Christian author, Merrill Tenney: "Bible survey is fundamental to all Bible study. If a student expects to comprehend any part or doctrine of the scriptures, he must know what they teach as a whole."

When using the survey method, we get a bird's-eye view and study entire Bible books to become acquainted with general information rather than the details of each verse. We investigate subjects like the author, when and where he was writing from, his style of writing, a book's theme, important topics contained in the book, who it was written for, and issues or circumstances the recipients might have been facing. Looking at the social, political, and spiritual background—as well as the chronology of events—helps to explain why certain events happened.

We can also survey the entire Old or New Testament so we understand how the books of the Bible are divided and relate to each other. The thirty-nine Old Testament books can be divided into five categories:

- Genesis through Deuteronomy, the first five books, are known as the Law or the Pentateuch (meaning five volumes).

- Joshua through Esther are the twelve historical books.

- Job through Song of Solomon are the five poetic books.

- Isaiah through Daniel are the five major prophets.

- Hosea through Malachi are the twelve minor prophets.

The Old Testament was originally written in Hebrew, with some small sections written in Aramaic. They deal primarily with God's relationship with His chosen nation, Israel.

The twenty-seven New Testament books, originally written in Greek, can be divided into four categories:

- The four Gospels and Acts are the historical books.
- Romans through Philemon, the next thirteen books, are letters of the apostle Paul to churches or individuals.
- Hebrews through Jude, the next eight books, are called the general letters.
- Revelation, a prophetic book, appropriately ends the New Testament.

Bible encyclopedias, Bible dictionaries, and Old and New Testament overviews are all helpful when surveying the Bible.

3. The Topical Method

It is important to develop a good grasp of the major topics and themes in scripture. We can learn many things about the great mysteries God has revealed about Himself, His Word, and His plan through the ages. He has revealed things about the unseen world of angels and demons, heaven and hell, and life and death.

Directly related to our lives are the subjects of mankind's personal sin and God's only way of salvation through His Son, Jesus Christ. And then there are specific topics from the Bible that interest us—questions relating to finances, prayer, or purpose.

To master these topics we need to accumulate all that the Bible says about them and then organize that information. A Bible concordance and a topical Bible can guide us to specific verses about subjects throughout the Bible. Then we can see how each subject is addressed in the Old Testament and the New Testament, and by individual biblical authors.

This method was especially helpful to me as a young Christian because, like many new believers, I had so many doctrinal questions I wanted answers to. One of the first study books I read was *Major Bible Themes* by Lewis Sperry Chafer (later revised by John Walvoord), explaining fifty-two Bible doctrines. I concentrated on particular subjects to better learn what God had to say about them and in doing this established a strong foundation for my faith. As I continued to study other topics, a Bible dictionary provided a nice introduction to each. A Bible encyclopedia also provided more extensive articles for the topics being studied.

Because so many individual verses are examined throughout scripture in the topical Bible study method, we must take care that the verses under consideration are understood in their proper context.

Additional resources that will prove helpful are *Nave's Topical Bible*, containing some twenty thousand topics, and an online study tool (I recommend *The New Topical Textbook* by R. A. Torrey at www.bible.topics.com) for finding Bible verses indexed by subject.

4. The Biographical Method

Individual people in the Bible are interesting—and developing character sketches about them will produce many valuable lessons. When you bring together bits and pieces in the Bible about a person's life, amazing pictures can emerge.

The Bible mentions over twenty-nine hundred people, some by name only. A concordance can be used to find every Bible verse in which a name is found, but care must be exercised since many Bible characters shared names. For example, six women in the Bible are named Mary, five men are named John, and five men are named James.

Remember, too, that some people are referred to by more than one name. At times, God assigned a new name to indicate a significant change in a person's circumstances. The elderly and childless couple Abram and Sarai had their names changed to Abraham and Sarah, indicating that they would eventually become the patriarch and matriarch of many nations and believers (Genesis 17:5, 15).

Young Daniel and his three friends Azariah, Mishael, and Azariah were forcibly abducted by the Babylonians, who changed their Hebrew names to names honoring false gods. Daniel (meaning "God is my judge") had his name changed to Belteshazzar (meaning "Bel protect the king"). Daniel's friends were renamed Shadrach, Meshach, and Abednego (Daniel 1:7).

In New Testament times, people were occasionally known more by their Roman than their Hebrew names. Saul was known as Paul (Acts 13:9); while John, who authored the second Gospel, was known as Mark (Acts 12:25). The apostle Peter, meanwhile, was known by three names that all appear together in many translations of John 1:42: Peter (his Greek name), Simon (his Hebrew name), and Cephas (his Aramaic name).

Through faith in God's power, as we see in Hebrews 11, believers have accomplished some amazing things. These Bible characters are examples for us, even in their weaknesses. David, the man after God's own heart, sinned in the matter of Uriah the Hittite (1 Kings 15:5). The apostle Peter denied the Lord (Matthew 26:69-74). Elijah was a man just like us (James 5:17).

This realization should encourage us. Through the experience of the real people of the Bible, we learn that God is forgiving and patient—that He is the God of second chances.

When developing a character sketch, studying books such as *All the Men of the Bible* and *All the Women of the Bible* (by Herbert Lockyer) or *Twelve Ordinary Men* and *Twelve Extraordinary Women* (by John MacArthur) may prove helpful.

As you pursue the biographical method of Bible study, honestly ponder the question, "What would God write about *my* life?"

5. *The Word Study Method*

When a person is new to the Christian faith, some terms may be unfamiliar. Words like *propitiation, redemption, imputation, justification,* and *sanctification* are basic to the "good news" message of God's salvation in scripture. The words of scripture are the words that God inspired, so they become part of our study. God wants us to understand them so that we can believe His truth and experience personal blessing as we apply it to our lives. By using a concordance, you'll be able to locate these words and see how they're used.

Several Greek words might be translated into one English word. Using study tools like *Strong's Exhaustive Concordance* and *Vine's Complete Expository Dictionary* is essential to understanding the variety of meanings. Let's consider a few examples.

The World

Three Greek words all translate into the English word *world.* The Greek word *kosmos* is used in John 3:16: "For God so loved the world that He gave His only begotten Son." This refers to the world order of unsaved people who are opposed to God and controlled by Satan. It is also used in Acts 17:24 to describe the orderliness of the material world that was created by God.

The Greek word *aion* is used in Romans 12:2: "And do not be conformed to this world." It refers to the particular age in which we live that's influential with false ideas and evil. J. B. Phillips translates this, "Don't let the world around you squeeze you into its mold," which is a warning against worldliness.

The Greek word *oikoumene* is used in Matthew 24:14: "And this gospel of the kingdom will be preached in all the world." Matthew is referring to the inhabited world of people who hear a worldwide Gospel proclamation.

Love

We use the English word *love* for three Greek words that have slightly different meanings. The conversation that the risen Lord Jesus had with Peter in John 21:15–19 uses two of the Greek words.

Since Peter denied knowing the Lord three times, Jesus asked Peter three times if he really loved Him. In the first two questions, Jesus uses the Greek word *agape,* which refers to self-sacrificing love (also used in John 3:16). In Peter's answer he uses another Greek word for love, *phileo*, which emphasizes only fondness, probably because he still feels too much shame to use the word emphasizing a total loving devotion.

When Jesus asks the same question for the third time, He questions even Peter's fondness for Him by also using the word that Peter did, *phileo*. This intentional change of Greek words by Jesus is missed in our English Bible, but it's the reason why Peter was grieved.

Day

Context also has an important bearing on the meaning of words. The word *day*, for example, as used in the Bible, has several meanings that are determined by the context. In Genesis 1:5 there are two meanings: the twelve hours of light are called *day*, and the twenty-four-hour period indicated by the repeated phrase "the evening and the morning" is also called *day*. When the word *day* appears with a numerical adjective (first day, second day), it consistently refers to a twenty-four-hour period. In Genesis 2:4, *day* also refers to the entire creative week. In Psalm 20:1, *day* refers to an indefinite period of time.

6. The Devotional Method

Many Christians use the phrase "having personal devotions" when referring to the devotional method. This type of study is less technical than the others and is primarily for personal inspiration and encouragement to deepen our relationship with God, drawing near to Him so that He might draw near to us. Bible reading, prayer, and perhaps reading a devotional book with a brief message are normally a part of devotions.

Three popular daily devotional booklets are *Our Daily Bread*, *Days of Praise*, and *Today in the Word*. Charles Spurgeon's *Morning and Evening* is a classic devotional tool that gives a message for the beginning of the day and one for the end of the day. Another classic is *My Utmost for His Highest* by Oswald Chambers.

Meditation is a normal part of the devotional method. This is the practice of pondering and reflecting on the meaning of God's words and works and their application to our lives. Anyone who has received a letter from a loved one who is far away understands the meaning of meditation. We read and reread the contents and then think about them. The psalmist said, "I will meditate on Your precepts, and contemplate Your ways" (Psalm 119:15).

Our meditation hopefully carries on throughout the day as we consider how God's Word applies to our particular daily activities. Blessing waits for those who delight in the law of the Lord and meditate on it day and night (Psalm 1:2).

Meditation can be greatly aided by memorization of God's Word. Being able to retrieve scripture from memory is useful when we're discouraged; we're able to ponder the uplifting promises of God. "I remembered Your judgments of old, O LORD, and have comforted myself" (Psalm 119:52).

When facing temptation like the Lord Jesus in Matthew 4, we use scripture that we have learned to be able to remain faithful. The psalmist said, "Your word I have hidden in my heart, that I might not sin against You" (Psalm 119:11).

Being a good witness to those who don't know the Lord requires being able to recall appropriate Gospel verses that will be spiritually helpful to them. Many believers have said to themselves following conversations with an unbeliever, "Oh, I wish I would have remembered that particular verse!" They're referring to verses they knew about that would have been helpful in the conversation but that they had never committed to memory.

The devotional method of study prepares us to meet each day with the knowledge that we have been redeemed by Christ and that He'll strengthen us to do His will.

READING THROUGH THE BIBLE

● ● ●

Having recommended six types of Bible study, I want to conclude this chapter by mentioning one more study activity that's advisable: reading through the Bible.

Bible reading should be an ongoing activity in the Christian life. I admire Christians who read through the Bible in one year, something I've never accomplished because I'm easily sidetracked by issues I come across in the text and prefer to investigate at that time. The result is I get behind in my reading schedule. My first attempt to read through the Bible took me five years. That's a lot of rabbit trails! My second time through the Bible took three years. So far, this has been my best attempt. If we have the attitude of Job, we'll stay in God's Word no matter how long it takes us to get through it. He said, "I have treasured the words of His mouth more than my necessary food" (Job 23:12).

Remember, the *activity* of Bible study is more important than the *method*, but learning to use these methods opens doors to discovering the great truths of scripture. As they say at Nike, "Just do it!"

COLLABORATION

• • •

USING BIBLE STUDY HELPS

---

*Bring the cloak that I left with Carpus at Troas when
you come—and the books, especially the parchments.*

2 TIMOTHY 4:13

Paul, as a Pharisee and as a Christian preacher, was a great student of scripture. No one actually knows what books he was asking Timothy to bring to him when he wrote. But there's a possibility that they were more than books of scripture, that they were books to help him in his own study of scripture.

In this chapter, I'll recommend Bible study tools that are helpful for "a worker" (2 Timothy 2:15). Every worker needs tools of the trade to do his job. The toolbox of Bible students is a personal library, and their tools are study books and helps that aid them in understanding the scriptures. The workshop is that special location where they study.

Study resources produced by Bible scholars give Christians the advantage of reading the insights that these servants of Christ have gained through their own study. Study books are valuable, but they must be kept in their place. They aren't inspired by God as scripture is. They aren't the final word on any biblical text. Our primary source of truth is the Bible. *Sola scriptura* was the Latin saying established during the Protestant Reformation that means "the Bible alone." By using that pronouncement, the Reformers established the Word of God as their only authority for doctrine and practice. God's Word is to be given its rightful place in our lives.

It has been my conviction that when Christians meet to worship and study on the Lord's Day, the Bible should be opened and taught. On rare occasions, I've been in places where a Sunday school manual has been opened in a class and then discussed while Bibles remained closed (though not mine, by the way). This kind of activity doesn't give the Bible its rightful place of priority in a public setting. Whether it's a public or private setting, we shouldn't give our study tools more attention than we give our Bible.

Christians must also beware of becoming -*ites*. These are believers who automatically accept everything that a certain Christian author says or writes. Church history tells the story of an estimated fifty thousand people in the 1840s known as Millerites. They were exclusive followers of the prophetic pronouncements of an influential Bible teacher, William Miller, who had set a date of October 22, 1844, for Christ's return to earth. Many prepared for the exciting day—but were greatly disappointed when it came and went with no sign of Jesus. This kind of sectarianism can lead to troublesome divisions among believers, even when truth is being taught.

This is an old problem addressed by even the apostle Paul when he asked the Corinthian church, "For when one says, 'I am of Paul,' and another, 'I am of Apollos,' are you not carnal?" (1 Corinthians 3:4). We all have our favorite authors and Bible teachers, but they should make this same point—that we should not be isolated followers of only certain individuals. God has blessed the church with many gifted people He wants to use for our blessing. So let's beware of the divisive spirit becoming an *-ite* can produce.

Some Christians have debated whether study books should even be used at all. They believe that only the Bible itself should be studied.

As a young, impressionable believer, I remember listening to a debate between two Christians in the church I attended who took opposing views on this. One said that God speaks only by His Spirit through the Bible and no study books should be used. This sounded very spiritual. The other believed that God could also use study books to aid our understanding of His Word. Who's right?

My wife and I now own over six hundred study books in our personal library. The Bible-only view is an attractive one economically, but I don't believe it's correct, because as stated earlier, God has gifted certain believers with the gift of teaching. This isn't referring to just a natural ability to teach others. This is a supernatural enablement given by God after salvation (1 Corinthians 12:11, 28).

The gifted teacher can minister through speaking and writing. The mode of getting the information isn't the issue. God uses mature believers to disciple other believers through direct contact in one-to-one or small-group interaction, and indirect contact through the printed page, tapes, CDs, and so on.

None of these resources eliminates the need for spending plenty of time in the Bible. Let's look at some available resources that can help us with our study of the Bible. Please note that the titles I mention are of books that I've used—some may now be out of print or updated under slightly different titles, but all are likely available from libraries, bookstores, or sellers of used books.

BIBLE STUDY HELPS

• • •

Study Bibles

As a new believer being invited to a home Bible class, I was amazed to see people with Bibles that had a wealth of additional study notes in them. I had never seen anything like them. I soon purchased a New Scofield Reference Bible. When this wore out years later, my next one was a Ryrie Study Bible. My wife uses a MacArthur Study Bible. Other people I know use the Life Application Study Bible. These are only a few in a long list of study Bibles now available in a variety of English translations.

One thing to remember is that the notes in study Bibles are the explanatory words of people, not the authoritative words of God. The study aids are provided as immediate helps and are not meant to be the end of our investigation. We shouldn't depend too heavily on just the explanations in our study Bibles. They'll have helpful introductions to each book of the Bible and outlines so we can see how books fit together. Explanatory notes about the text, doctrine, and Christian living appear on every page. Some study Bibles have charts, articles, extensive cross-references, a concordance, a topical index, and numerous maps.

Bible Dictionaries and Encyclopedias

Among the first tools we need are Bible dictionaries and encyclopedias. They have more than just the definitions of words. They contain brief articles on major Bible subjects with helpful explanations and scripture references related to the subject. These books cover a spectrum of subjects from A to Z, making them a reference tool that gets used repeatedly. I recommend *The New Unger's Bible Dictionary*, *Zondervan's Pictorial Bible Dictionary*, and *The International Standard Bible Encyclopedia*, a five-volume set.

Exhaustive Concordances

An exhaustive concordance lists every reference where every biblical word is found. When you can remember only a few words of a verse, you can look up one of the words and this book helps you find its reference. Often, in the back, you'll also find an English dictionary for Old Testament Hebrew words and New Testament Greek words. It's important to make sure the concordance you use is keyed to the Bible translation you use. *Strong's Exhaustive Concordance* is keyed to the King James Version. After my Bible, I use this tool more than any other resource that I have.

Bible Atlases

For those who want a more detailed description of geography in the Bible with explanatory articles, this is the book to use. Atlases contain many more maps than those that appear in the backs of Bibles. This resource won't be used as frequently as others, but it helps to better understand locations and travel in Bible times.

Expository Dictionaries

When studying words of the Bible, use an expository dictionary. A Webster's English dictionary is fine as far as it goes, but it primarily deals with English. We're dealing with English translations of Greek words when we study the New Testament. This study aid examines the original Greek words used in verses and then gives a brief definition and explanation of the word. It also has select references to where the Greek word appears in the New Testament. I recommend *Vine's Expository Dictionary of Old and New Testament Words* by W. E. Vine.

Topical Bibles

Topical Bibles list biblical words alphabetically and give select references to where the word you are looking for is found. Many times the entire verse is written out so you can read the verse in the book. Larger subjects are broken down into subcategories so you can find verses with a particular emphasis. For example, in Nave's Topical Bible, the word *faith* has the following subheadings: faith enjoined; faith exemplified; faith in Christ; the trial of faith. Use this resource when you're doing word studies or character sketches.

Commentaries

This is my favorite category of study helps. Most of the books I own are commentaries. Using these books is like being taught by great men and women of God.

Some are expository in nature, explaining individual verses and analyzing how they fit together. These generally include an outline of the entire book of the Bible.

Other commentaries are more devotional, emphasizing lessons for Christian living.

Some are technical in nature, working closely with the original languages.

After you read several commentaries, you'll soon discover that the books with more pages are normally more helpful because they address more issues. Difficult questions that arise are usually addressed, including possible solutions.

A personal benefit from reading commentaries written by Bible scholars is that you're able to test your own conclusions against what the experts are saying.

This obviously requires that you interact with the Bible text yourself before consulting a commentary. Remember, we're learning how to study the Bible, not learning how to study commentaries.

Commentaries aren't the final word about any text. Even Bible scholars disagree at times. My humble experience has been that I find myself not agreeing with any Bible commentator one hundred percent of the time. My guess is that this is the conclusion of most serious students of the Bible.

Books that have been helpful to me are single books that cover the entire Bible like *Jamieson, Fausset, and Brown's Commentary on the Whole Bible* (that's one book!). Sets that cover the entire New Testament or the entire Bible (which provide greater detail) include the six-volume set of Matthew Henry commentaries; *The Bible Knowledge Commentary* by Walvoord and Zuck, a two-volume set; and *The Bible Exposition Commentary* by Warren Wiersbe, a six-volume set. Much larger sets are *The New Testament Commentary* series by Hendriksen and Kistemaker and the *MacArthur New Testament Commentary* series.

One of the first things to find out about authors is their theological persuasion. Some write from a dispensational perspective while others write from the Reformed perspective. This is good to know ahead of time because there are doctrinal differences in the content of the books. Your pastor should be able to help with this and make suggestions about what to buy.

AUDIO SERMONS

Sermons are available on CDs and online. Listening to sermons is a way to increase your knowledge by using leisure time. If you spend a lot of time traveling and aren't using the time for other things, you can listen to hours of Bible messages. You can also listen to Bible teachers while you're taking care of projects in your home or yard.

One very helpful website, which allows you to listen to hundreds of sermons, is www.sermonaudio.com. You can search the available recordings by scripture reference, topic, or speaker.

GETTING BIBLE STUDY RESOURCES

• • •

I want to say a few things about where to get Bible study tools. Every Christian should own a few basic study books. To develop your personal library, make a wish list of the books you need. I've learned the hard way not to buy books I'm not acquainted with. The money I used to buy ten books that weren't that good could have been used to buy one good book. Add the study tools to your library that are valuable to you. Get recommendations from Christians who you believe can help you with this project and then visit your local Christian bookstore or an Internet bookseller.

You can also borrow Bible study books from your church library or even many public libraries. If the public library lacks a title you're seeking, it might be able to order the book from another library.

The Internet offers a wealth of free Bible study tools. People frequently comment that when they get on the Internet they use up so much time—if this is your case, you might want to use that time for studying the Bible online.

Here's a list of websites in random order with brief descriptions. There is much more on these sites than what's in the descriptions. There are also links to other Bible study sites. When you find a website that's helpful to you, put the link into a Bible study file in your Favorites so you can visit the site repeatedly.

bible.org

You'll find articles by topic or by passage. They have online Bible dictionaries, concordances, encyclopedias, and an extensive question-and-answer section. Click the STUDY drop-down to utilize the site's Bible study tool, Lumina.

studylight.org

At the top of the page, click BIBLE STUDY TOOLS to find commentaries, concordances, dictionaries, and encyclopedias.

preceptaustin.org

Click on SITE INDEX for an alphabetical listing of this entire website. Type any Bible word into the search box to find numerous articles about the word. Bible commentaries with verse-by-verse exposition, dictionaries, and maps are available.

Biblos.com

This Bible study website was formed in 2007 with a mission to increase the visibility of and accessibility to the scriptures by providing free online access to Bible study tools in many languages and to promote the Gospel of Christ through learning, study, and application of God's Word.

Biblestudytools.com

This website is a large Bible study toolbox that provides over thirty Bible translations with an amazing "compare translations" tab. Also available are numerous Bible commentaries, encyclopedias, and dictionaries. You'll find an extensive list of daily devotionals that can be searched by topic or author. A topical study tool is available, as well as a long list of classic sermons. The "video" link shows numerous Christian leaders answering biblical questions.

ourdailybread.org

This is the website of Our Daily Bread Ministries. At the homepage you'll find the information available in more than a dozen languages. Numerous online daily devotionals are available. The strength of this site is the availability of over two hundred Bible-based teachings in easy-to-read, thirty-two-page booklets that can be viewed online or requested as printed copies.

e-sword.net

This site provides free, downloadable Bible study software. Numerous Bible translations are available along with Bible commentaries, dictionaries, encyclopedias, topical Bibles, and a concordance. It is so popular, it has been accessed from some 225 countries around the world.

Any of these Bible study resources can be helpful in your personal study.

GETTING ORGANIZED

● ● ●

My last suggestion is that you save and file your own notes from your study of the scriptures. Get two three-ring binders to hold your study notes. One notebook can be used for study notes by Bible topics, and the other one can be used for study notes by Bible references. It's a blessing to see and read later what God has taught you in your own study of His Word.

MOTIVATION

• • •

PUTTING THOUGHTS INTO ACTION

*You therefore, beloved, knowing this beforehand, be on your guard
so that you are not carried away by the error of unprincipled men
and fall from your own steadfastness, but grow in the grace and
knowledge of our Lord and Savior Jesus Christ. To Him be
the glory, both now and to the day of eternity. Amen.*

2 PETER 3:17-18 NASB

The following ad appeared in the South Central Telephone Company Yellow Pages: "Born to be battered. . .the loving phone call book. Underline it, circle things, write in the margins, turn down page corners—the more you use it, the more valuable it gets to be."

If that's true of a phone book, think how much truer it is of God's Word!

Many people have made their Bibles "personal" by the comments they've written in them year after year. It's hard for some people to think about replacing their old Bibles with new ones even if they're falling apart—because they've found such wisdom, comfort, and power in the pages they've studied and cherished for years.

Alan Redpath, the pastor of Moody Church in Chicago from 1953 to 1962, advised believers to "wreck" their Bibles every ten years. He meant to wear them out by constant use. I once saw a message on a church sign that read, "A Bible that is falling apart is usually owned by someone who isn't." This is a point well taken.

I imagine most believers would say that reading and studying the Bible is a good thing to do. Virtually all Christian families in the United States own at least one Bible. The Bible is repeatedly the bestselling book every year. . .but perhaps still one of the least read. Why the disconnect? The answer has both a human dimension and a spiritual one.

HINDRANCES TO BIBLE STUDY

● ● ●

From a human perspective, the busyness of life can keep us from scripture. Sometimes we can be lazy when it comes to our spiritual health and responsibilities. And sometimes we simply don't understand how important Bible study actually is. It needs to be viewed as a personal priority and implemented as part of our daily routine, just like any other activity we see as important.

From a spiritual perspective, sin in our lives can keep us from spending time in the Word. We can lose our spiritual appetite for the knowledge of God. The forces of darkness are doing all they can to keep us from studying God's truth. Any activity that uses up our time will do—it doesn't have to be evil, just something that weighs us down and takes our time.

We might ask, "Isn't going to church enough? Isn't reading and studying the Bible what pastors and Sunday school teachers do?" It's true that this is a large part of what pastors and teachers are to do, but it's also what everyone in a church congregation is supposed to do. Pastor Alistair Begg has said that his job as a pastor isn't just to feed the sheep, but to teach them how to cook!

Learning God's truth through reading and studying the Bible is something He wants for us. Consider these verses, all of which we've already referenced:

*Now these [Bereans] were more noble-minded than those in
Thessalonica, for they received the word with great eagerness,
examining the Scriptures daily to see whether these things were so.*
ACTS 17:11 NASB

*For whatever was written in earlier
times was written for our instruction.*
ROMANS 15:4 NASB

*Study to shew thyself approved unto God, a workman that
needeth not to be ashamed, rightly dividing the word of truth.*
2 TIMOTHY 2:15 KJV

Verses like these should motivate us to be in our Bibles. Believers generally agree that the will of God includes gathering regularly with God's people to worship and pray, living a life of faith and obedience, serving the Lord and spreading His Gospel—but how many add that studying the Bible is also the will of God? Is this optional or essential?

As he ended his second letter, the apostle Peter strongly urged believers to "grow. . .in the knowledge of our Lord and Savior Jesus Christ" (2 Peter 3:18), something that starts with knowing His Word.

Believers who are growing in knowledge of God's truth have made a conscious decision to study the Word. Seek out those people who know a lot about the Bible, and ask them about their own study habits—then imitate their examples. We are all given the same twenty-four hours a day. You might consider rising earlier in the morning or eliminating a television show or two in the evening. Devote even a small amount of time to Bible study, and add to it as the pursuit becomes a regular habit in your life.

Just like eating, studying the Bible is a lifelong activity. We'll never get to the point where we've learned all that there is to know about God's Word, then be able to stop. Our spirit needs God's Word every day just like our bodies need food.

It's wise to make your study time a matter of prayer. We pray about many things, and this subject is important to God, too. It's no accident that God allowed you to be born at this time with all the advantages we have to learn His Word. Pray about your Bible study every day, because "the prayer of the upright is His delight" (Proverbs 15:8).

Our adversary, the devil, does all he can to keep us from obeying God's will. God wants to bless us, and the devil wants to destroy us. If we as believers fall away from our Bible study, it might seem unimportant to us at the time. But we can be sure that the forces of darkness are celebrating and planning new ways to attack us.

When Jesus defeated Satan's temptation in the wilderness, Luke says, "The devil. . .departed from Him until an opportune time" (Luke 4:13). The devil leaves us for only a brief time. He always returns with different temptations until he finds what's effective against us. Satan knows that Christians, without regular time in the Bible, become weak and ineffective for Christ. But with prayer and the sword of the Spirit—the Word of God—we can overcome this enemy of our souls, enjoying our time with God as we feed on His Word.

GOD'S GOODNESS

● ● ●

God's goodness should stir us to study His Word. His goodness is revealed in our lives in a variety of ways.

The Roman emperor Diocletian persecuted Christians during his reign. In AD 303 he ordered Bibles to be confiscated and burned. Many were destroyed. Today, in countries hostile to the Christian faith, simply owning a Bible is a crime. In our country we have no obstacles like this. Have you ever pondered the blessing that

Bibles are legal in our country and so liberally available to us?

The Bible is also available to us in our language. The International Bible Society says the Bible or parts of it have been translated into about twenty-five hundred of the world's sixty-five hundred languages. The majority of language groups have never read the Bible, and its life-giving words about Jesus Christ, in their own language. It's a sad reality that millions of people still have never heard that blessed name.

In some countries where Bibles are permitted, there aren't enough copies for everyone who wants one. In many places, Bibles are shared by believers so they can each read the Word briefly. In other places, a believer who owns a Bible may be asked to become the pastor of a group simply because no one else has access to the Word.

Imagine the hardship of not having Bibles in our worship services. One of the great joys I have as a Bible teacher is to say, "Let's open our Bibles together." Because of the goodness of God, we don't face the limitations of many fellow Christians around the world. We should acknowledge these blessings by gratefully and faithfully studying the Bible.

Over the years, I've been blessed by numerous men and women of God, pastors, and missionaries who have exemplified love for and diligent pursuit of the scriptures. I've appreciated people in church congregations who have also had an impact on me. Let me tell you about three of them.

1. The example of Eleanor

A dignified elderly widow, Eleanor, who is now with the Lord, attended multiple church services and home Bible classes each week to hear the Word of the Lord being taught. When it came to scripture, she seemed to have the energy of a young person. The Bible was the book of her life. When we talked, we would always end up discussing God's Word.

I'll never forget visiting her home to drop off a few Bible sermons on cassette tape. She mentioned that she was doing a personal study on the Gospel of Mark and showed me the six Bible commentaries that she was working through. I was amazed that she'd go to so much effort in a personal study, but she was serious about learning God's Word. At the time, I was still learning what it meant to love God's Word, and Eleanor's example made me want the same kind of energy and excitement for the Bible.

2. The example of a man who couldn't read

An older gentleman, who crossed my path only momentarily, left a lasting impression. He was a little man who briefly attended the same home Bible class that I did. He was a quaint, soft-spoken man, always dressed in a suit and tie. During discussions, it was obvious that he knew a lot about the Bible.

One night, the teacher asked him to read a verse aloud. He paused, hung his head, and admitted he didn't know how to read. I was stunned, as I'm sure everyone else was, too. How could someone who lacked reading skills know so much about the Bible? Obviously, he'd listened to other people teach the Bible—a lot.

The fact that this man overcame the obstacle of illiteracy and still learned the Bible is what struck me. When people are determined to learn God's Word, He'll provide the help they need.

3. The example of Amy

The third person is a wife and stay-at-home mom named Amy. Where is the mother of three young children going to find the time to study the Bible?

To add to this challenge, Amy has been legally blind since her teen years. Can a person with obvious time restraints and the obstacle of partial blindness still study the Bible? The answer is yes, though it requires a great amount of determination and love for God's Word.

Using a powerful magnifying glass, Amy studies scripture for an entire hour—and at times an hour and a half—while two of her children are at school and her youngest takes a nap. That is the quiet time God has provided for her. The example of these three believers inspires me. And I'm guessing God has put similar people in your life to serve as examples to you. The apostle Paul once said, "Imitate me, just as I also imitate Christ" (1 Corinthians 11:1). On another occasion he wrote, "Brethren, join in following my example, and note those who so walk, as you have us for a pattern" (Philippians 3:17). Value these kinds of people in your life. Imitate the good that you see in them. Thank God that He has brought them into your life. Pray that you'll be a better Christian for having known them.

MARY AND MARTHA

• • •

As we conclude, let's consider the lives of Mary and Martha of Bethany. Mary is a great biblical example of a person whose desire was to be taught by Jesus: every time she appears in the Bible, she's kneeling before Him. In John 11, she's at His feet in sorrow. In John 12, she's at His feet in adoration. In Luke 10, she's at His feet to learn truth. Mary, the worshipper, wants her soul fed by Jesus—her sister Martha, the worker, wants to feed Jesus.

Mary and Martha had welcomed Jesus into their home. With good intentions, Martha took steps to prepare a meal for the honored guest. Then Mary is introduced into the story: "And she had a sister called Mary, who also sat at Jesus' feet and heard His word" (Luke 10:39). Martha was in the kitchen cooking food, and Mary was in the living room, learning from Jesus. Martha, annoyed that Mary wasn't helping with the work, interrupted the Lord, saying, "Lord, do You not care that my sister has left me to serve alone? Therefore tell her to help me" (Luke 10:40).

Jesus, in His divine wisdom, analyzed the situation and told Martha she was filled with unnecessary anxiety that had harmfully affected her priorities. The things she worried about really weren't important. "One thing is needed," Jesus told Martha, "and Mary has chosen that good part, which will not be taken away from her" (Luke 10:42).

Jesus commended Mary for having good priorities, namely, learning the Word of God. Bible expositor G. Campbell Morgan calls this "the one supreme necessity."

Mary's experience was that of being taught by the incarnate Christ. Each of us can experience the blessing of being taught by the risen Christ—by the power of His Holy Spirit, through the study of God's amazing Word.

• • •

Grow in the grace and knowledge of our Lord and Savior Jesus Christ.
To Him be the glory, both now and to the day of eternity. Amen.

2 PETER 3:18 NASB

APPENDICES

A.

OUTLINE FOR THE EXPOSITIONAL METHOD

Due to its brevity, the New Testament book of Philemon makes for good practice on the expositional method of Bible study.

You'll discover in this personal letter from the apostle Paul to a Christian friend that each individual verse is vitally connected to the others. The book contains the great themes of forgiveness and reconciliation in a historical setting where slavery (an integral part of the story) was an accepted way of life. Onesimus, a runaway slave, had fled from his Christian master, Philemon. Paul shows that through Christian truth the institution of slavery can be transformed from the inside out.

This book study can help people who need to experience forgiveness and reconciliation in their own lives.

Below, I will attempt to start you on an expositional study of Philemon. Practice on this small book, then try other passages by yourself!

Step 1

Compile your Bible study tools—a Bible, Bible dictionary, pen or pencil, and paper. I also advise you to commit to a regular time of day to study.

Step 2

At the tops of blank note pages, write the verse references and the words of the verses in full sentences—that is, if a sentence continues over multiple verses, show an entire sentence on a note page. If a sentence is too long for a single note page, carry it over onto a second or third page. Continue this process until every verse you're studying is accounted for on your note pages, and leave the remainder of each page for your own study notes.

In the case of Philemon, the book's twenty-five verses actually contain sixteen sentences (in the New King James Version), so you'll have sixteen pages for study notes, plus one additional page for developing of an outline of the entire book.

In expositional studying you'll want to look beyond the verse numbers and focus on entire sentences. Study the way you speak—in complete sentences. This helps to overcome our tendency to focus on favorite verses, perhaps out of context, while ignoring less prominent but equally important verses nearby.

Now, read your selected section of scripture repeatedly, acquainting yourself with all the information found in the text. With each reading, slow down and look more closely to discover things you may have overlooked previously. Reading multiple Bible versions can be helpful in this process.

Step 3

Write your observations about each verse. Record your findings, and ask "who, what, when, where, why, and how?" Look for the key words that connect thoughts—and for reoccurring words that emphasize a theme.

Keeping first things first, be careful to write only what is actually stated in the text. Your personal thoughts can be recorded later. (You might want to note the difference by using two headings: "What is stated" and "Additional thoughts and lessons.")

Group sentences together by their most common thought, and give each grouping a title. You should now be able to identify a single theme as the title of the entire portion of scripture you are studying.

Step 4

Try your own study of the first three verses of Philemon as an exercise. Once you're done, compare your notes with the example study notes provided on page 60, consulting Bible commentaries and other study resources as well. Keep at it, to refine and improve your own Bible study skills

SCRIPTURE PASSAGE ....

....

....

WHAT IS STATED ....

....

....

....

....

....

....

....

....

....

ADDITIONAL THOUGHTS ....

....

....

....

....

....

....

Additional Expositional Notes pages appear on pp. 76-97

EXAMPLE EXPOSITIONAL STUDY NOTES

SCRIPTURE PASSAGE

PHILEMON 1-3 (Use your Bible translation of choice.)

WHAT IS STATED

v. 1   The letter's authors are named and described as Paul, a prisoner of Christ, and Timothy, a brother to all. The letter's first and main recipient, Philemon, is described two ways, as "our beloved friend and fellow laborer."

v. 2   Three additional recipients are named and described—Apphia the beloved ("our sister," ESV), Archippus our fellow soldier, and the congregation that meets in Philemon's house.

v. 3   The first sentence (vv. 1-3) ends with a traditional greeting common in Paul's letters desiring divine blessing on the recipients. In this case, grace and peace have specific reference to the trouble caused by Onesimus.

ADDITIONAL THOUGHTS

v. 1   Paul begins this letter by immediately referring to his troubling circumstances of imprisonment (Acts 27-28) and connects this to Christ's providence and later as something experienced for His cause—"my chains for the gospel" (v. 13). This letter is called one of Paul's "prison epistles" written while under guard by the Roman authorities. The main characters in this story are obvious by how many times they're referred to. Paul speaks of himself at least twenty-two times, Philemon twenty-six times (though only naming him once), Onesimus the slave eight times, and Christ, the indispensable Person who makes these kinds of forgiveness stories possible, eleven times. This personal letter to Philemon was an open letter for everyone. Philemon's response to Onesimus will eventually affect everyone in his life.

v. 2   Because of their association with Philemon, Apphia (a feminine name) may be Philemon's wife while Archippus may be his son and/or a key church leader. Cross references indicate that Philemon is a wealthy member of the Colossian church and hosts church meetings in his large home (Colossians 4:7-9, 17). Therefore the epistles to the Colossians and Philemon are closely connected.

B.

OUTLINE FOR THE TOPICAL METHOD

The step-by-step method of topical Bible study is very similar to both the biographical and word-study methods. I'll use a topical study example in the pages following.

What differs is that the topical method of Bible study focuses more on doctrinal issues and important themes, while biographical studies concentrate on people and word studies on particular terms and phrases.

In the following example of topical Bible study, we'll examine the apostle Paul's customary greeting that appears with slight variations at the beginning of each of his thirteen New Testament letters. This greeting, which was common in Paul's day, was deepened with Christian thought.

Paul's salutation in Romans 1:7 reads like this: "Grace to you and peace from God our Father and the Lord Jesus Christ." The two spiritual qualities found in this greeting—grace and peace—will be investigated topically.

The following study will use only selected texts to get you started, leaving many others for your own additional pursuit. God has revealed so much about these two great themes that you will be able to find entire books written on each. For your own topical study, try the following steps.

Step 1

Compile your Bible study tools—a Bible, Bible dictionary, Bible encyclopedia, topical Bible and/or concordance, and writing materials.

Step 2

Write the definition of your topic from a Bible dictionary (rather than an English dictionary), since you'll see your topic from the biblical languages and in a biblical context. Later, as you begin to study Bible verses on your topic, your understanding of its definition should blossom.

Step 3

Compile all the essential scripture texts related to your topic by using a topical Bible and/or concordance. Then, as you read the verses, group texts together into separate categories of emphasis. Select a title that best describes each set of verses that you've grouped together.

Step 4

Write your observations about what each verse actually says about your topic. Be sure to distinguish between what the verse states and your own personal thoughts. You might want to use headings like "What is stated" and "Additional thoughts."

Step 5

Try your own study of the topic of grace as an exercise. Once you're done, compare your notes with the example study notes provided on pages 65-66, consulting Bible commentaries and other study resources as well. Keep at it, to refine and improve your own Bible study skills!

TOPIC AND DEFINITION ....

....

....

SCRIPTURE REFERENCE ....

WHAT IS STATED ....

....

....

....

....

....

ADDITIONAL THOUGHTS ....

....

....

....

....

....

....

....

....

....

SCRIPTURE REFERENCE ....

WHAT IS STATED ....

....

....

....

....

....

ADDITIONAL THOUGHTS...

....

....

....

....

....

....

....

....

....

....

....

....

*Additional Topical Notes pages appear on pp. 98-119

EXAMPLE TOPICAL STUDY NOTES

TOPIC AND DEFINITION

Grace. The definition according to *Baker's Evangelical Dictionary of Biblical Theology* states in part, "An accurate, common definition describes grace as the unmerited favor of God toward man." The *Our Daily Bread* devotional puts it this way: "Grace is everything for nothing to those who don't deserve anything." A suggested acronym for grace is "God's Riches At Christ's Expense," which adds the important thought of God's favor coming through Christ's sacrifice—though that still doesn't fully convey all that grace means.

As seen in the following verses, God's grace is first experienced in salvation. Then it continues to operate throughout our entire Christian life as we "grow in grace." Finally, in heaven, we'll continue to experience "the exceeding riches of His grace" (Ephesians 2:7). Thus, the Christian message is rightly called "the gospel of the grace of God" (Acts 20:24).

SCRIPTURE REFERENCE

Numbers 6:25

WHAT IS STATED

"The LORD. . .be gracious to you." These words are part of a benediction that Jewish priests were to announce during worship services to the nation of Israel revealing that God was gracious to His people.

ADDITIONAL THOUGHTS

The words of this benediction surely laid a foundation for Paul's customary New Testament greetings. There were many Old Testament expressions of God's grace and uses of this word, beginning with Noah (Genesis 6:8), heard in a self-proclamation by the Lord to Moses (Exodus 34:6-9), and expressed in song by the sons of Korah (Psalm 84:11), while Proverbs 3:34 is quoted in the New Testament in James 4:6.

SCRIPTURE REFERENCE

John 1:14-17

WHAT IS STATED

In v. 14, Jesus—the incarnate Word of God—was personally "full of grace and truth," which was visible to His followers. An older edition of the New International Version conveys the truth of v. 16 beautifully: "From the fullness of his grace we have all received one blessing after another." Like waves coming into the shore one after another, a constant flow of blessings was the daily experience of Jesus' followers.

Finally, v. 17 contrasts Moses, who gave the law (which was to reveal God's righteous standards and show man his sin), with Jesus Christ, through whom came saving "grace and truth" with the fullness of blessings.

ADDITIONAL THOUGHTS

Saving grace: This aspect of grace is related to the conversion of sinners to Christ.

C.

OUTLINE FOR THE BIOGRAPHICAL METHOD

In the following step-by-step example, we'll examine the lives of Aquila and Priscilla, a Christian couple found in the New Testament. It should prove to be an easy study since their names are always listed together—and found in only six verses.

Married believers and single people thinking about marriage will discover great lessons in this study touching on both marital and spiritual life.

Let's begin with three steps that will always be used in this type of study.

Step 1

Choose your character for study and assemble the following tools: your Bible, an exhaustive concordance, pens or pencils, and blank paper. A Bible atlas may be helpful in this study due to its frequent geographical references.

Step 2

Using a concordance, locate all the Bible verses in which the person's name is found. Remember that sometimes a name is common to multiple individuals—or the same person may have different names—so take care that the verses you select are all about the right person.

Write the references on your paper, leaving plenty of space between each so you can record your own observations. You'll want to examine the immediate context of each of your selected verses to locate additional information that may be pertinent to your study. If you discover something interesting, write those references also.

Step 3

Reread each verse several times to see what is actually stated about the person being studied. Take your time, and ask "who, what, when, where, why, and how?"

Though there may not be an answer to each of the "five Ws," they will assist you in seeing everything that is clearly stated in the verses you've chosen—and may lead to other considerations later in your study.

As always, it is very important to make a clear distinction in your notes between what is actually stated in verses and what may only be implied. Deal primarily with what is actually stated so you don't read something into the scriptures. (Remember, we cannot improve on what God has said, as Psalm 19:7 states: "The law of the LORD is perfect.") When scripture is silent, it's best to simply accept the fact that God hasn't revealed everything to us.

We will note this difference below by using the headings "What is stated" and "Additional thoughts."

Step 4

Once you have completed your biographical study notes, you'll want to arrange them logically. I have two recommendations:

First, you can use all or part of the following outline for answering significant questions. This outline can be adjusted to fit the amount of material that God has revealed in the Bible about the person you're studying:

1. Their calling in life—what is stated about their birth, family, job, community, service for God, etc.?
2. Their communion with God—what was their relationship to God?
3. The chronology of their life—what were the different stages of their life?
4. The character of their life—what kind of person were they?
5. Their companions—who were the other people in their life?
6. The conclusion—what major themes and Bible verses best summarizes their life?

Second, you can organize your material in chronological order—which is the way the selected verses on pages 70-72 are arranged.

Step 5

Try your own study of Aquila and Priscilla as an exercise. Once you're done, compare your notes with the study notes provided on pages 70-72, consulting Bible commentaries and other study resources as well. Keep at it, to refine and improve your own Bible study skills!

CHARACTER(S) AND REFERENCE..

WHAT IS STATED ....

....

....

....

....

....

ADDITIONAL THOUGHTS..

....

....

....

....

....

....

....

....

....

....

....

*Additional Biographical Notes pages appear on pp. 120–141

EXAMPLE BIOGRAPHICAL STUDY NOTES

CHARACTER(S) AND REFERENCE

Aquila and Priscilla; Acts 18:2 (context, 18:1-3)—"Aquila. . .had recently come from
Italy with his wife Priscilla."

WHAT IS STATED

v. 1   Paul was temporarily traveling alone (Acts 17:15-16) from Athens on his
second mission trip and met this couple for the first time in the city of
Corinth, Greece.

v. 2   Aquila had a Jewish heritage, but both he and his wife are known only
by their Roman names. Scripture is silent about Priscilla's ethnic origin.
Aquila was born in the Gentile region of Pontus near the Black Sea. They
had recently traveled to Corinth, having fled Rome since all Jews had
been banished from that city by the Roman emperor.

v. 3   Because they were all experienced tent makers, they did manual labor
together in a small business. Paul worked with them and stayed with them
as they opened their home to him.

ADDITIONAL THOUGHTS

vv. 1-2 Aquila means "eagle," which was used as a symbol in the Roman military.
But because of his Jewish background he could associate his name with
favorite Bible verses like Exodus 19:4 and Isaiah 40:31 that describe what
God does for His people. The name Priscilla has a suggested meaning of
"ancient," which she could associate with the nature of God described in
Isaiah 46:10 and Daniel 7:9.

   Both parties traveled from different cities and ended up in the same
place. Their story indicates that God providentially brought them together
to work for Him (Proverbs 3:5-6; 16:9). This couple would eventually
be able to say that their trial of being forced from their home in Rome
turned out to be a blessing in disguise as they came to be personally
acquainted with Paul. God was working all things together for their good
(Romans 8:28).

v. 3   The original meeting of these parties was in a business and occupational setting. Paul worked part-time as needed to support himself financially. This was the beginning of a close and lasting friendship between them as Paul not only worked with them and lived with them, but also served the Lord with them. Having the apostle Paul in your home at the end of each day's work would have been an edifying experience as he discussed the scriptures and what God was accomplishing through his Bible teaching ministry in Corinth (18:11).

CHARACTER(S) AND REFERENCE

Aquila and Priscilla; Acts 18:18 (context, 18:18-19)—"Priscilla and Aquila were with him."

WHAT IS STATED

v. 18   After eighteen months in Corinth, Paul decided it was time for him to leave the new church he had planted and finish his mission trip. He left by boat and was accompanied by this couple.

v. 19   They had a layover in the seaport city of Ephesus. Paul then left this couple there as he continued his journey to Jerusalem and then back to his sending home church in Antioch, Syria (vv. 21-22).

ADDITIONAL THOUGHTS

v. 18   This couple packed their bags to move again, but this time for the cause of the Gospel. We are not told when they became Christians, but it's obvious at this point that they are devoted believers who have joined Paul in his mission work.

v. 19   It appears to be a strategic move by Paul to leave this couple in Ephesus. He planned to return there on his next mission trip, and left them behind to establish a Christian testimony in the community through their personal lives, their business, and a nucleus of new believers forming that would lay a foundation for the famous Ephesian church described in Acts 19.

CHARACTER(S) AND REFERENCE

Aquila and Priscilla; Acts 18:26 (context, 18:24-28)—"Aquila and Priscilla heard him. . ."

WHAT IS STATED

vv. 24-25 Apollos, who was Jewish and a gifted itinerant Bible teacher, visited Ephesus. He was raised in the famous city of Alexandria, Egypt, which was known for its Grecian educational center.

v. 26 While hearing him teach the Old Testament, this couple detected a deficiency in his message that is not stated. They initiated a private meeting with him to explain "the way of God" more accurately. It proved to be a fruitful meeting (vv. 27-28).

v. 27 When Apollos prepared to continue his travels, the brethren—which surely included this well-known couple—gave him a letter of recommendation.

ADDITIONAL THOUGHTS

v. 26 This couple was diligent in business, which is time consuming—but they maintained a personal priority of always growing together in knowledge of God's Word as they discussed the scriptures together. Their influence reached into the business world and church life—and now, with unified and humble voices, they reached into the theological arena as they were able to respectfully persuade a renowned teacher to improve his Gospel message. In their minds, eloquence and enthusiasm in teaching were no substitute for accuracy.

v. 27 This letter of recommendation was designed to protect churches from false teachers and advance the credentials of Apollos.

RECOMMENDED BIBLE CHARACTERS TO STUDY

Many diverse people in the Bible are worthy of a closer look. The following list—including both men and women—shows some of the amazing people who by their lives teach great lessons for our Christian lives today.

Old Testament Men

1. Abraham—He became a father in his old age—and the father of all believers.
2. Isaac—He was the miracle child born to Abraham—and offered to God on an altar.
3. Jacob (Israel)—He was born as a twin and lived as a trickster, yet experienced the saving grace of God.
4. Job—He was the man who lost everything but his faith and is remembered for his perseverance.
5. Moses—He was born a Hebrew slave, educated as an Egyptian prince, spoke with God face-to-face, and led God's people to the promised land.
6. Samson—This warrior-judge was known for his supernatural strength and moral weakness.
7. Samuel—As a young child he was given back to God by his mother to be raised by Eli the priest—and became God's prophet.
8. David—This shepherd boy defeated a giant, served a king, wrote psalms, and later became a king himself.
9. Daniel—He survived abduction to a foreign country and a night in a lions' den, becoming an advisor to kings and a prophet to God's people.
10. Jonah—This missionary prophet ran from God, was swallowed by a great fish, and returned to initiate a revival in a foreign country.

Old Testament Women

1. Sarah—The wife of Abraham miraculously had a child in her old age and became the matriarch of all faithful women.
2. Rebekah—Through God's direction she left her family to become the wife of a man she had never met.
3. Rachel—The woman of a real love story; Jacob worked fourteen years for her father to be able to marry her.
4. Miriam—She helped save her baby brother, Moses, but he could not save her in Israel's wilderness wanderings.
5. Hannah—God answered the prayer of this barren woman who eventually gave birth to a son whom she named Samuel—meaning "God heard."

6. Rahab—This prostitute from the pagan city of Jericho was saved and is listed in the genealogy of the Messiah.
7. Ruth—One book of the Bible tells the story of this proselyte woman who became a widow and was remarried to her kinsman-redeemer.
8. Esther—This Jewish girl became a Persian queen who was used providentially to save her people.
9. Deborah—As a courageous prophet and judge, she was Israel's only female military leader.
10. The good wife—A mother describes to her son the ideal woman to look for as a wife in the poem of Proverbs 31.

New Testament Men

1. James—This half brother of Jesus grew up as an unbeliever—but later in life followed Jesus and became a church leader.
2. Peter—This man left his family fishing business to become the leader of Jesus' twelve apostles.
3. Nicodemus—This Pharisee is known for his conversation with Jesus about being "born again."
4. Paul—He was a zealous enemy of the Gospel who later became an emissary for the Gospel—and authored most of the books of the New Testament.
5. Barnabas—This man was given this nickname because of the encouraging character he exemplified when he accepted the recently converted Paul and introduced him to Jesus' apostles.
6. Luke—He was a physician who accompanied Paul on mission trips—and the only Gentile to write scripture.
7. Silas (Silvanus)—This Jerusalem church leader was selected by Paul as a replacement for John Mark on Paul's second mission trip.
8. Timothy—This young man was trained by Paul and helped write many of his New Testament letters. Two letters from Paul are also addressed to him.
9. Stephen—He was a Christian apologist who became the first church martyr.
10. Philemon—This prominent Christian was encouraged by Paul to take back his now-converted runaway slave as a brother in Christ.

New Testament Women

1. Mary, mother of Jesus—This young virgin was selected by God to miraculously give birth to God's Son.
2. Elizabeth—She miraculously gave birth in her old age to a son later known as John the Baptist.

3. Anna—This widow, who served God for decades in the temple, saw the Christ before her death.
4. Mary Magdalene—This demon-possessed woman was delivered by Christ to become His follower.
5. Mary of Bethany—When this woman is named in scripture, she is always seen at Jesus' feet.
6. The woman at the well—This immoral woman, called by some "the bad Samaritan," had a lengthy conversation with Jesus about living water.
7. The mother of Rufus—This woman's motherly instincts made such an impact on the apostle Paul that he referred to her as his mother.
8. Lydia—This businesswoman became one of the first converts in the new Philippian church.
9. Dorcas (Tabitha)—This charitable woman was miraculously raised from the dead by the apostle Peter.
10. Lois and Eunice—Timothy's faithful grandmother and mother together raised him to honor the Lord.

SCRIPTURE PASSAGE

....

....

WHAT IS STATED

....

....

....

....

....

....

....

ADDITIONAL THOUGHTS

....

....

....

....

....

....

SCRIPTURE PASSAGE...

....

....

WHAT IS STATED ....

....

....

....

....

....

....

....

....

ADDITIONAL THOUGHTS...

....

....

....

....

....

....

....

SCRIPTURE PASSAGE ....

....

....

WHAT IS STATED ....

....

....

....

....

....

....

....

ADDITIONAL THOUGHTS ....

....

....

....

....

....

....

....

SCRIPTURE PASSAGE...

....

....

WHAT IS STATED ....

....

....

....

....

....

....

....

....

ADDITIONAL THOUGHTS..

....

....

....

....

....

....

....

SCRIPTURE PASSAGE..

....

....

WHAT IS STATED ....

....

....

....

....

....

....

....

....

ADDITIONAL THOUGHTS..

....

....

....

....

....

....

....

SCRIPTURE PASSAGE ....

....

....

WHAT IS STATED ....

....

....

....

....

....

....

....

....

ADDITIONAL THOUGHTS ....

....

....

....

....

....

....

SCRIPTURE PASSAGE ....

....

....

WHAT IS STATED ....

....

....

....

....

....

....

....

ADDITIONAL THOUGHTS ....

....

....

....

....

....

....

SCRIPTURE PASSAGE ....

....

....

WHAT IS STATED ....

....

....

....

....

....

....

....

ADDITIONAL THOUGHTS ....

....

....

....

....

....

....

....

SCRIPTURE PASSAGE...

....

....

WHAT IS STATED ....

....

....

....

....

....

....

....

ADDITIONAL THOUGHTS...

....

....

....

....

....

....

SCRIPTURE PASSAGE ....

....

....

WHAT IS STATED ....

....

....

....

....

....

....

....

ADDITIONAL THOUGHTS ....

....

....

....

....

....

....

....

SCRIPTURE PASSAGE

....

....

WHAT IS STATED

....

....

....

....

....

....

....

....

ADDITIONAL THOUGHTS

....

....

....

....

....

....

....

SCRIPTURE PASSAGE

WHAT IS STATED

ADDITIONAL THOUGHTS

SCRIPTURE PASSAGE..

....

....

WHAT IS STATED...

....

....

....

....

....

....

....

....

ADDITIONAL THOUGHTS..

....

....

....

....

....

....

....

SCRIPTURE PASSAGE ....

....

....

WHAT IS STATED ....

....

....

....

....

....

....

....

....

ADDITIONAL THOUGHTS ....

....

....

....

....

....

....

....

SCRIPTURE PASSAGE ....

....

....

WHAT IS STATED ....

....

....

....

....

....

....

....

ADDITIONAL THOUGHTS ....

....

....

....

....

....

....

SCRIPTURE PASSAGE

WHAT IS STATED

ADDITIONAL THOUGHTS

SCRIPTURE PASSAGE

....

....

WHAT IS STATED

....

....

....

....

....

....

....

....

....

ADDITIONAL THOUGHTS

....

....

....

....

....

....

....

SCRIPTURE PASSAGE..

....

....

WHAT IS STATED ....

....

....

....

....

....

....

....

....

ADDITIONAL THOUGHTS..

....

....

....

....

....

....

SCRIPTURE PASSAGE...

....

....

WHAT IS STATED ....

....

....

....

....

....

....

....

....

ADDITIONAL THOUGHTS...

....

....

....

....

....

....

SCRIPTURE PASSAGE

WHAT IS STATED

ADDITIONAL THOUGHTS

SCRIPTURE PASSAGE

....

....

WHAT IS STATED

....

....

....

....

....

....

....

....

ADDITIONAL THOUGHTS

....

....

....

....

....

....

....

SCRIPTURE PASSAGE ....

....

....

WHAT IS STATED ....

....

....

....

....

....

....

....

....

....

ADDITIONAL THOUGHTS ....

....

....

....

....

....

....

....

TOPIC AND DEFINITION ....

....

....

SCRIPTURE REFERENCE ....

WHAT IS STATED ....

....

....

....

....

ADDITIONAL THOUGHTS ....

....

....

....

....

....

....

....

....

SCRIPTURE REFERENCE ....

WHAT IS STATED ....

....

....

....

....

....

ADDITIONAL THOUGHTS...

....

....

....

....

....

....

....

....

....

....

....

....

TOPIC AND DEFINITION ....

....

....

SCRIPTURE REFERENCE ....

WHAT IS STATED ....

....

....

....

....

....

ADDITIONAL THOUGHTS ....

....

....

....

....

....

....

....

....

....

SCRIPTURE REFERENCE ....

WHAT IS STATED ....

....

....

....

....

....

ADDITIONAL THOUGHTS...

....

....

....

....

....

....

....

....

....

....

....

TOPIC AND DEFINITION ....

....

....

SCRIPTURE REFERENCE ....

WHAT IS STATED ....

....

....

....

....

....

ADDITIONAL THOUGHTS...

....

....

....

....

....

....

....

....

....

SCRIPTURE REFERENCE ....

WHAT IS STATED ....

....

....

....

....

....

ADDITIONAL THOUGHTS ....

....

....

....

....

....

....

....

....

....

....

....

....

TOPIC AND DEFINITION ....

....

....

SCRIPTURE REFERENCE ....

WHAT IS STATED ....

....

....

....

....

....

ADDITIONAL THOUGHTS ....

....

....

....

....

....

....

....

....

....

SCRIPTURE REFERENCE ....

WHAT IS STATED ....

....

....

....

....

....

ADDITIONAL THOUGHTS ....

....

....

....

....

....

....

....

....

....

....

....

TOPIC AND DEFINITION ....

....

....

SCRIPTURE REFERENCE ....

WHAT IS STATED ....

....

....

....

....

....

ADDITIONAL THOUGHTS ....

....

....

....

....

....

....

....

....

....

SCRIPTURE REFERENCE ....

WHAT IS STATED ....

....

....

....

....

....

ADDITIONAL THOUGHTS ....

....

....

....

....

....

....

....

....

....

....

TOPIC AND DEFINITION ....

....

....

SCRIPTURE REFERENCE ....

WHAT IS STATED ....

....

....

....

....

....

ADDITIONAL THOUGHTS ....

....

....

....

....

....

....

....

....

....

SCRIPTURE REFERENCE ....

WHAT IS STATED ....

....

....

....

....

....

ADDITIONAL THOUGHTS ....

....

....

....

....

....

....

....

....

....

....

....

TOPIC AND DEFINITION ....

....

....

SCRIPTURE REFERENCE ....

WHAT IS STATED ....

....

....

....

....

....

ADDITIONAL THOUGHTS ....

....

....

....

....

....

....

....

....

....

SCRIPTURE REFERENCE ....

WHAT IS STATED ....

....

....

....

....

....

ADDITIONAL THOUGHTS ....

....

....

....

....

....

....

....

....

....

....

....

....

TOPIC AND DEFINITION ....

....

....

SCRIPTURE REFERENCE ....

WHAT IS STATED ....

....

....

....

....

....

ADDITIONAL THOUGHTS ....

....

....

....

....

....

....

....

....

SCRIPTURE REFERENCE ....

WHAT IS STATED ....

....

....

....

....

....

ADDITIONAL THOUGHTS..

....

....

....

....

....

....

....

....

....

....

....

TOPIC AND DEFINITION ....

....

....

SCRIPTURE REFERENCE ....

WHAT IS STATED ....

....

....

....

....

....

ADDITIONAL THOUGHTS ....

....

....

....

....

....

....

....

....

....

SCRIPTURE REFERENCE ....

WHAT IS STATED ....

....

....

....

....

....

ADDITIONAL THOUGHTS ....

....

....

....

....

....

....

....

....

....

....

....

....

....

TOPIC AND DEFINITION ....

....

....

SCRIPTURE REFERENCE ....

WHAT IS STATED ....

....

....

....

....

....

ADDITIONAL THOUGHTS ....

....

....

....

....

....

....

....

....

....

SCRIPTURE REFERENCE ....

WHAT IS STATED ....

....

....

....

....

....

ADDITIONAL THOUGHTS...

....

....

....

....

....

....

....

....

....

....

....

TOPIC AND DEFINITION ....

....

....

SCRIPTURE REFERENCE ....

WHAT IS STATED ....

....

....

....

....

....

ADDITIONAL THOUGHTS ....

....

....

....

....

....

....

....

....

....

SCRIPTURE REFERENCE ....

WHAT IS STATED ....

....

....

....

....

....

ADDITIONAL THOUGHTS ....

....

....

....

....

....

....

....

....

....

....

....

....

....

CHARACTER(S) AND REFERENCE ....

WHAT IS STATED ....

....

....

....

....

....

ADDITIONAL THOUGHTS ....

....

....

....

....

....

....

....

....

....

....

....

....

CHARACTER(S) AND REFERENCE...

WHAT IS STATED ....

....

....

....

....

....

ADDITIONAL THOUGHTS...

....

....

....

....

....

....

....

....

....

....

....

....

CHARACTER(S) AND REFERENCE..

WHAT IS STATED ....

....

....

....

....

....

ADDITIONAL THOUGHTS..

....

....

....

....

....

....

....

....

....

....

....

....

CHARACTER(S) AND REFERENCE ....

WHAT IS STATED ....

....

....

....

....

....

ADDITIONAL THOUGHTS ....

....

....

....

....

....

....

....

....

....

....

....

CHARACTER(S) AND REFERENCE..

WHAT IS STATED ....

....

....

....

....

....

ADDITIONAL THOUGHTS...

....

....

....

....

....

....

....

....

....

....

....

....

CHARACTER(S) AND REFERENCE..

WHAT IS STATED ....

....

....

....

....

....

ADDITIONAL THOUGHTS..

....

....

....

....

....

....

....

....

....

....

....

CHARACTER(S) AND REFERENCE..

WHAT IS STATED ....

....

....

....

....

....

ADDITIONAL THOUGHTS...

....

....

....

....

....

....

....

....

....

....

....

....

CHARACTER(S) AND REFERENCE...

WHAT IS STATED ....

....

....

....

....

....

ADDITIONAL THOUGHTS...

....

....

....

....

....

....

....

....

....

....

....

CHARACTER(S) AND REFERENCE...

WHAT IS STATED ....

....

....

....

....

....

ADDITIONAL THOUGHTS..

....

....

....

....

....

....

....

....

....

....

....

....

CHARACTER(S) AND REFERENCE ....

WHAT IS STATED ....

....

....

....

....

....

ADDITIONAL THOUGHTS ....

....

....

....

....

....

....

....

....

....

....

....

....

CHARACTER(S) AND REFERENCE...

WHAT IS STATED ....

....

....

....

....

....

ADDITIONAL THOUGHTS..

....

....

....

....

....

....

....

....

....

....

....

CHARACTER(S) AND REFERENCE..

WHAT IS STATED ....

....

....

....

....

....

ADDITIONAL THOUGHTS..

....

....

....

....

....

....

....

....

....

....

....

....

CHARACTER(S) AND REFERENCE ....

WHAT IS STATED ....

....

....

....

....

....

ADDITIONAL THOUGHTS ....

....

....

....

....

....

....

....

....

....

....

....

....

CHARACTER(S) AND REFERENCE...

WHAT IS STATED ....

....

....

....

....

....

ADDITIONAL THOUGHTS...

....

....

....

....

....

....

....

....

....

....

....

CHARACTER(S) AND REFERENCE ....

WHAT IS STATED ....

....

....

....

....

....

ADDITIONAL THOUGHTS ....

....

....

....

....

....

....

....

....

....

....

....

....

CHARACTER(S) AND REFERENCE..

WHAT IS STATED ....

....

....

....

....

....

ADDITIONAL THOUGHTS...

....

....

....

....

....

....

....

....

....

....

....

....

CHARACTER(S) AND REFERENCE ....

WHAT IS STATED ....

....

....

....

....

....

ADDITIONAL THOUGHTS ....

....

....

....

....

....

....

....

....

....

....

....

....

CHARACTER(S) AND REFERENCE...

WHAT IS STATED ....

....

....

....

....

....

ADDITIONAL THOUGHTS...

....

....

....

....

....

....

....

....

....

....

....

....

CHARACTER(S) AND REFERENCE...

WHAT IS STATED ....

....

....

....

....

....

ADDITIONAL THOUGHTS...

....

....

....

....

....

....

....

....

....

....

....

....

CHARACTER(S) AND REFERENCE...

WHAT IS STATED ....

....

....

....

....

....

ADDITIONAL THOUGHTS...

....

....

....

....

....

....

....

....

....

....

....

....

CHARACTER(S) AND REFERENCE..

WHAT IS STATED ....

....

....

....

....

....

ADDITIONAL THOUGHTS..

....

....

....

....

....

....

....

....

....

....

....

CHARACTER(S) AND REFERENCE..

WHAT IS STATED ....

....

....

....

....

....

ADDITIONAL THOUGHTS...

....

....

....

....

....

....

....

....

....

....

....

DATE..

TITLE/SUBJECT ....

SCRIPTURE REFERENCE(S)..

NOTES/INSIGHTS ....

....

....

....

....

....

....

....

....

....

....

....

....

HOW THIS STUDY APPLIES TO MY LIFE ....

....

....

....

DATE..

TITLE/SUBJECT ....

SCRIPTURE REFERENCE(S)..

NOTES/INSIGHTS ....

....

....

....

....

....

....

....

....

....

....

....

HOW THIS STUDY APPLIES TO MY LIFE ....

....

....

....

DATE..

TITLE/SUBJECT ....

SCRIPTURE REFERENCE(S)..

NOTES/INSIGHTS ....

....

....

....

....

....

....

....

....

....

....

....

....

HOW THIS STUDY APPLIES TO MY LIFE ....

....

....

....

DATE

TITLE/SUBJECT

SCRIPTURE REFERENCE(S)

NOTES/INSIGHTS

HOW THIS STUDY APPLIES TO MY LIFE

DATE..

TITLE/SUBJECT ....

SCRIPTURE REFERENCE(S)..

NOTES/INSIGHTS ....

....

....

....

....

....

....

....

....

....

....

....

HOW THIS STUDY APPLIES TO MY LIFE ....

....

....

....

DATE ....

TITLE/SUBJECT ....

SCRIPTURE REFERENCE(S) ....

NOTES/INSIGHTS ....

....

....

....

....

....

....

....

....

....

....

....

....

HOW THIS STUDY APPLIES TO MY LIFE ....

....

....

....

DATE..

TITLE/SUBJECT ....

SCRIPTURE REFERENCE(S)..

NOTES/INSIGHTS ....

....

....

....

....

....

....

....

....

....

....

....

HOW THIS STUDY APPLIES TO MY LIFE ....

....

....

....

DATE..

TITLE/SUBJECT ....

SCRIPTURE REFERENCE(S)..

NOTES/INSIGHTS ....

....

....

....

....

....

....

....

....

....

....

....

....

....

HOW THIS STUDY APPLIES TO MY LIFE ....

....

....

....

DATE ....

TITLE/SUBJECT ....

SCRIPTURE REFERENCE(S)..

NOTES/INSIGHTS ....

....

....

....

....

....

....

....

....

....

....

....

....

HOW THIS STUDY APPLIES TO MY LIFE ....

....

....

....

DATE..

TITLE/SUBJECT ....

SCRIPTURE REFERENCE(S)..

NOTES/INSIGHTS ....

....

....

....

....

....

....

....

....

....

....

....

....

HOW THIS STUDY APPLIES TO MY LIFE ....

....

....

....

DATE ....

TITLE/SUBJECT ....

SCRIPTURE REFERENCE(S) ....

NOTES/INSIGHTS ....

....

....

....

....

....

....

....

....

....

....

....

....

....

....

HOW THIS STUDY APPLIES TO MY LIFE ....

....

....

....

DATE ....

TITLE/SUBJECT ....

SCRIPTURE REFERENCE(S) ....

NOTES/INSIGHTS ....

....

....

....

....

....

....

....

....

....

....

....

....

HOW THIS STUDY APPLIES TO MY LIFE ....

....

....

....

DATE..

TITLE/SUBJECT ....

SCRIPTURE REFERENCE(S)..

NOTES/INSIGHTS ....

....

....

....

....

....

....

....

....

....

....

....

....

....

HOW THIS STUDY APPLIES TO MY LIFE ....

....

....

....

DATE ....

TITLE/SUBJECT ....

SCRIPTURE REFERENCE(S) ....

NOTES/INSIGHTS ....

....

....

....

....

....

....

....

....

....

....

....

....

HOW THIS STUDY APPLIES TO MY LIFE ....

....

....

....

DATE..

TITLE/SUBJECT ....

SCRIPTURE REFERENCE(S)..

NOTES/INSIGHTS ....

....

....

....

....

....

....

....

....

....

....

....

....

....

....

HOW THIS STUDY APPLIES TO MY LIFE ....

....

....

....

DATE ....

TITLE/SUBJECT ....

SCRIPTURE REFERENCE(S) ....

NOTES/INSIGHTS ....

....

....

....

....

....

....

....

....

....

....

....

HOW THIS STUDY APPLIES TO MY LIFE ....

....

....

....

DATE..

TITLE/SUBJECT ....

SCRIPTURE REFERENCE(S)...

NOTES/INSIGHTS ....

....

....

....

....

....

....

....

....

....

....

....

....

HOW THIS STUDY APPLIES TO MY LIFE ....

....

....

....

DATE ....

TITLE/SUBJECT ....

SCRIPTURE REFERENCE(S) ....

NOTES/INSIGHTS ....

....

....

....

....

....

....

....

....

....

....

....

HOW THIS STUDY APPLIES TO MY LIFE ....

....

....

....

DATE ....

TITLE/SUBJECT ....

SCRIPTURE REFERENCE(S) ....

NOTES/INSIGHTS ....

....

....

....

....

....

....

....

....

....

....

....

....

....

HOW THIS STUDY APPLIES TO MY LIFE ....

....

....

....

DATE...

TITLE/SUBJECT ....

SCRIPTURE REFERENCE(S)..

NOTES/INSIGHTS ....

....

....

....

....

....

....

....

....

....

....

....

....

HOW THIS STUDY APPLIES TO MY LIFE ....

....

....

....

DATE..

TITLE/SUBJECT ....

SCRIPTURE REFERENCE(S)..

NOTES/INSIGHTS ....

....

....

....

....

....

....

....

....

....

....

....

HOW THIS STUDY APPLIES TO MY LIFE ....

....

....

....

DATE..

TITLE/SUBJECT ....

SCRIPTURE REFERENCE(S)...

NOTES/INSIGHTS ....

....

....

....

....

....

....

....

....

....

....

....

....

....

HOW THIS STUDY APPLIES TO MY LIFE ....

....

....

....

DATE...

TITLE/SUBJECT ....

SCRIPTURE REFERENCE(S)..

NOTES/INSIGHTS ....

....

....

....

....

....

....

....

....

....

....

....

HOW THIS STUDY APPLIES TO MY LIFE ....

....

....

....

DATE..

TITLE/SUBJECT ....

SCRIPTURE REFERENCE(S)..

NOTES/INSIGHTS ....

....

....

....

....

....

....

....

....

....

....

....

HOW THIS STUDY APPLIES TO MY LIFE ....

....

....

....

DATE..

TITLE/SUBJECT ....

SCRIPTURE REFERENCE(S)..

NOTES/INSIGHTS ....

....

....

....

....

....

....

....

....

....

....

....

....

....

HOW THIS STUDY APPLIES TO MY LIFE ....

....

....

....

DATE...

TITLE/SUBJECT ....

SCRIPTURE REFERENCE(S)..

NOTES/INSIGHTS ....

....

....

....

....

....

....

....

....

....

....

....

HOW THIS STUDY APPLIES TO MY LIFE ....

....

....

....

DATE...

TITLE/SUBJECT ....

SCRIPTURE REFERENCE(S)..

NOTES/INSIGHTS ....

....

....

....

....

....

....

....

....

....

....

....

HOW THIS STUDY APPLIES TO MY LIFE ....

....

....

....

DATE...

TITLE/SUBJECT ....

SCRIPTURE REFERENCE(S)..

NOTES/INSIGHTS ....

....

....

....

....

....

....

....

....

....

....

....

....

HOW THIS STUDY APPLIES TO MY LIFE ....

....

....

....

DATE..

TITLE/SUBJECT ....

SCRIPTURE REFERENCE(S)..

NOTES/INSIGHTS ....

....

....

....

....

....

....

....

....

....

....

....

HOW THIS STUDY APPLIES TO MY LIFE ....

....

....

....

DATE...

TITLE/SUBJECT ....

SCRIPTURE REFERENCE(S)..

NOTES/INSIGHTS ....

....

....

....

....

....

....

....

....

....

....

....

....

HOW THIS STUDY APPLIES TO MY LIFE ....

....

....

....

DATE...

TITLE/SUBJECT ....

SCRIPTURE REFERENCE(S)..

NOTES/INSIGHTS ....

....

....

....

....

....

....

....

....

....

....

....

HOW THIS STUDY APPLIES TO MY LIFE ....

....

....

....

DATE ....

TITLE/SUBJECT ....

SCRIPTURE REFERENCE(S) ....

NOTES/INSIGHTS ....

....

....

....

....

....

....

....

....

....

....

....

....

HOW THIS STUDY APPLIES TO MY LIFE ....

....

....

....

DATE...

TITLE/SUBJECT ....

SCRIPTURE REFERENCE(S)..

NOTES/INSIGHTS ....

....

....

....

....

....

....

....

....

....

....

....

....

HOW THIS STUDY APPLIES TO MY LIFE ....

....

....

....

DATE..

TITLE/SUBJECT ....

SCRIPTURE REFERENCE(S)...

NOTES/INSIGHTS ....

....

....

....

....

....

....

....

....

....

....

....

....

HOW THIS STUDY APPLIES TO MY LIFE ....

....

....

....

DATE..

TITLE/SUBJECT ....

SCRIPTURE REFERENCE(S)..

NOTES/INSIGHTS ....

....

....

....

....

....

....

....

....

....

....

....

HOW THIS STUDY APPLIES TO MY LIFE ....

....

....

....

DATE..

TITLE/SUBJECT ....

SCRIPTURE REFERENCE(S)...

NOTES/INSIGHTS ....

....

....

....

....

....

....

....

....

....

....

....

HOW THIS STUDY APPLIES TO MY LIFE ....

....

....

....

DATE..

TITLE/SUBJECT ....

SCRIPTURE REFERENCE(S)..

NOTES/INSIGHTS ....

....

....

....

....

....

....

....

....

....

....

....

....

....

HOW THIS STUDY APPLIES TO MY LIFE ....

....

....

....

DATE ....

TITLE/SUBJECT ....

SCRIPTURE REFERENCE(S)...

NOTES/INSIGHTS ....

....

....

....

....

....

....

....

....

....

....

....

HOW THIS STUDY APPLIES TO MY LIFE ....

....

....

....

DATE..

TITLE/SUBJECT ....

SCRIPTURE REFERENCE(S)...

NOTES/INSIGHTS ....

....

....

....

....

....

....

....

....

....

....

....

....

HOW THIS STUDY APPLIES TO MY LIFE ....

....

....

....

DATE ....

TITLE/SUBJECT ....

SCRIPTURE REFERENCE(S) ....

NOTES/INSIGHTS ....

....

....

....

....

....

....

....

....

....

....

....

HOW THIS STUDY APPLIES TO MY LIFE ....

....

....

....

DATE..

TITLE/SUBJECT ....

SCRIPTURE REFERENCE(S)..

NOTES/INSIGHTS ....

....

....

....

....

....

....

....

....

....

....

....

....

HOW THIS STUDY APPLIES TO MY LIFE ....

....

....

....

DATE..

TITLE/SUBJECT ....

SCRIPTURE REFERENCE(S)..

NOTES/INSIGHTS ....

....

....

....

....

....

....

....

....

....

....

....

....

HOW THIS STUDY APPLIES TO MY LIFE ....

....

....

....

DATE...

TITLE/SUBJECT ....

SCRIPTURE REFERENCE(S)..

NOTES/INSIGHTS ....

....

....

....

....

....

....

....

....

....

....

....

....

HOW THIS STUDY APPLIES TO MY LIFE ....

....

....

....

DATE..

TITLE/SUBJECT ....

SCRIPTURE REFERENCE(S)...

NOTES/INSIGHTS ....

....

....

....

....

....

....

....

....

....

....

....

....

HOW THIS STUDY APPLIES TO MY LIFE ....

....

....

....

DATE..

TITLE/SUBJECT ....

SCRIPTURE REFERENCE(S)...

NOTES/INSIGHTS ....

....

....

....

....

....

....

....

....

....

....

....

....

....

HOW THIS STUDY APPLIES TO MY LIFE ....

....

....

....

DATE..

TITLE/SUBJECT ....

SCRIPTURE REFERENCE(S)...

NOTES/INSIGHTS ....

....

....

....

....

....

....

....

....

....

....

....

HOW THIS STUDY APPLIES TO MY LIFE ....

....

....

....

DATE...

TITLE/SUBJECT ....

SCRIPTURE REFERENCE(S)..

NOTES/INSIGHTS ....

....

....

....

....

....

....

....

....

....

....

....

....

....

HOW THIS STUDY APPLIES TO MY LIFE ....

....

....

....

DATE ....

TITLE/SUBJECT ....

SCRIPTURE REFERENCE(S) ....

NOTES/INSIGHTS ....

....

....

....

....

....

....

....

....

....

....

....

HOW THIS STUDY APPLIES TO MY LIFE ....

....

....

....

DATE ....

TITLE/SUBJECT ....

SCRIPTURE REFERENCE(S) ....

NOTES/INSIGHTS ....

....

....

....

....

....

....

....

....

....

....

....

HOW THIS STUDY APPLIES TO MY LIFE ....

....

....

....

DATE .....

TITLE/SUBJECT .....

SCRIPTURE REFERENCE(S) .....

NOTES/INSIGHTS .....

.....

.....

.....

.....

.....

.....

.....

.....

.....

.....

.....

.....

.....

HOW THIS STUDY APPLIES TO MY LIFE .....

.....

.....

.....

DATE...

TITLE/SUBJECT ....

SCRIPTURE REFERENCE(S)..

NOTES/INSIGHTS ....

....

....

....

....

....

....

....

....

....

....

....

....

HOW THIS STUDY APPLIES TO MY LIFE ....

....

....

....

DATE...

TITLE/SUBJECT ....

SCRIPTURE REFERENCE(S)..

NOTES/INSIGHTS ....

....

....

....

....

....

....

....

....

....

....

....

....

....

HOW THIS STUDY APPLIES TO MY LIFE ....

....

....

....

DATE..

TITLE/SUBJECT ....

SCRIPTURE REFERENCE(S)..

NOTES/INSIGHTS...

....

....

....

....

....

....

....

....

....

....

....

....

HOW THIS STUDY APPLIES TO MY LIFE ....

....

....

....

DATE...

TITLE/SUBJECT ....

SCRIPTURE REFERENCE(S)..

NOTES/INSIGHTS ....

....

....

....

....

....

....

....

....

....

....

....

....

HOW THIS STUDY APPLIES TO MY LIFE ....

....

....

....

DATE..

TITLE/SUBJECT ....

SCRIPTURE REFERENCE(S)..

NOTES/INSIGHTS ....

....

....

....

....

....

....

....

....

....

....

....

....

HOW THIS STUDY APPLIES TO MY LIFE ....

....

....

....

DATE..

TITLE/SUBJECT ....

SCRIPTURE REFERENCE(S)...

NOTES/INSIGHTS ....

....

....

....

....

....

....

....

....

....

....

....

....

HOW THIS STUDY APPLIES TO MY LIFE ....

....

....

....

DATE..

TITLE/SUBJECT ....

SCRIPTURE REFERENCE(S)...

NOTES/INSIGHTS ....

....

....

....

....

....

....

....

....

....

....

....

....

HOW THIS STUDY APPLIES TO MY LIFE ....

....

....

....

DATE ....

TITLE/SUBJECT ....

SCRIPTURE REFERENCE(S) ....

NOTES/INSIGHTS ....

....

....

....

....

....

....

....

....

....

....

....

HOW THIS STUDY APPLIES TO MY LIFE ....

....

....

....

DATE...

TITLE/SUBJECT ....

SCRIPTURE REFERENCE(S)..

NOTES/INSIGHTS ....

....

....

....

....

....

....

....

....

....

....

....

....

HOW THIS STUDY APPLIES TO MY LIFE ....

....

....

....

DATE..

TITLE/SUBJECT ....

SCRIPTURE REFERENCE(S)..

NOTES/INSIGHTS ....

....

....

....

....

....

....

....

....

....

....

....

....

HOW THIS STUDY APPLIES TO MY LIFE ....

....

....

....

DATE..

TITLE/SUBJECT ....

SCRIPTURE REFERENCE(S)...

NOTES/INSIGHTS ....

....

....

....

....

....

....

....

....

....

....

....

....

HOW THIS STUDY APPLIES TO MY LIFE ....

....

....

....

DATE..

TITLE/SUBJECT ....

SCRIPTURE REFERENCE(S)..

NOTES/INSIGHTS ....

....

....

....

....

....

....

....

....

....

....

....

....

....

HOW THIS STUDY APPLIES TO MY LIFE ....

....

....

....

DATE..

TITLE/SUBJECT ....

SCRIPTURE REFERENCE(S)..

NOTES/INSIGHTS ....

....

....

....

....

....

....

....

....

....

....

....

....

HOW THIS STUDY APPLIES TO MY LIFE ....

....

....

....

DATE..

TITLE/SUBJECT ....

SCRIPTURE REFERENCE(S)...

NOTES/INSIGHTS ....

....

....

....

....

....

....

....

....

....

....

....

....

....

HOW THIS STUDY APPLIES TO MY LIFE ....

....

....

....

DATE..

TITLE/SUBJECT ....

SCRIPTURE REFERENCE(S)..

NOTES/INSIGHTS ....

....

....

....

....

....

....

....

....

....

....

....

....

HOW THIS STUDY APPLIES TO MY LIFE ....

....

....

....

DATE..

TITLE/SUBJECT ....

SCRIPTURE REFERENCE(S)...

NOTES/INSIGHTS ....

....

....

....

....

....

....

....

....

....

....

....

....

....

HOW THIS STUDY APPLIES TO MY LIFE ....

....

....

....

DATE..

TITLE/SUBJECT ....

SCRIPTURE REFERENCE(S)..

NOTES/INSIGHTS ....

....

....

....

....

....

....

....

....

....

....

....

....

HOW THIS STUDY APPLIES TO MY LIFE ....

....

....

....